ABOUT THE AUTHOR.

Simon Morrell spent most of his life suffering in a dark cave of anxiety. As a child and into his early adulthood, he was the victim of bullies which escalated into unprovoked violent assaults.

This led to Simon developing full blown agoraphobia, panic attacks and a nervous breakdown. Scared of his own shadow, Simon turned to the Martial Arts and Karate for some solace and it was here he found his path in life.

He became a very successful Martial Artist and his qualifications include being a 6th Dan Black Belt at Practical Karate and Kick-Boxing, a Qualified Wrestling Coach (BAWA), a Registered Senior Self-Protection Instructor with The British Combat Association and a National Competitor and a Black Belt at Krav Maga Israeli Unarmed Combat. He has twice been awarded into the Hall of Fame.

He has attended and successfully completed training in Close Protection, Surveillance and Close Quarter Combat, and is the Chief Instructor of Fight Fortress Worldwide Inc.

His Black Belts were awarded after tests under some of the World's leading Martial Artists, including Alfie Lewis, Geoff Thompson and Peter Consterdine.

Today, he teaches his findings at his own centre in North Wales. He has been asked by an American organization to re-locate to the States and head a brand new academy there.

Most of his students come to Simon because they themselves have struggled with fear control and violent attack, and realise Simon can identify with them.

FROM BULLIED TO BLACK BELT

THE FIGHTBACK

A True Story.

A journey through agoraphobia, fear, violent assaults and a triumphant recovery.

By

Simon Morrell

Edited by James Eccles with an introduction by Geoff Thompson.

All photographs; Copyright Simon Morrell 2001-2014©

Published by Blue Porch Publishing.

ISBN 978-0-9565603-4-6

REGISTERED IN THE U.S. COPYRIGHT OFFICE, LIBRARY OF CONGRESS NO. PA0001849528

FROM BULLIED TO BLACK BELT

THE FIGHTBACK

A True Story

This version printed April 2014 (revised and updated)

Printed in Nov 2001 (1st edition) From Bullied To Black Belt

Reprinted Dec 2007 (2nd edition) From Bullied To Black Belt

Simon's website is www.simonmorrell.com.

He can be contacted at info@simonmorrell.com

He is available for motivational talks, seminars and self-defence training. His latest course 'Despite the Fear' © is about to be unleashed on an unsuspecting public! Be the first to book this life changing experience for your club, group, corporation or event.

DEDICATIONS

This is, as always, to Julie.

"Come in she said, I'll give you shelter from the storm"

And the song that always makes me think of her:

"If I Should Fall Behind, Wait For Me"

(Bruce Springsteen)

Which falling behind I do quite often!

There is not another person I would rather have by my side in a small war or crisis. Her strength is unbelievable. She bought me back from my dark place. Thank you and I love you.

This is also for my brilliant children, Luka Jake, Cy Tyson and Billy The Kid! My finest sparring partners.

ACKNOWLEDGEMENTS

Thanks to:-

I am not the first, and I am sure I will not be the last, to thank Geoff Thompson for his friendship, support and letting me use his strength when I had none left. Thank you for being a good friend to myself and my family. Without his encouragement I don't know where I would be right now. Also to the legendary Alfie Lewis whose encouragement and friendship has been magnificent.

I would like to thank all my friends in the Martial Arts world for the help, friendship and love they give me.

Thank you to James 'Jimmy' Eccles

Most of all, thanks to all the people who bullied all those years ago. You made me what I am! Congratulations!

Author's notes.

I wrote the first edition of From Bullied To Black Belt in 2001. A friend told me it would be a long process…he was right. Some thirteen years on I still consider it a work in progress. A work in progress in that the subject matter, anxiety entwined in violence coupled with panic and people's lack of code, is still prevalent today as is the ever present bullying. I think there are so many more people this story needs to reach and so the work in progress continues as we bring it into different media formats. As Social Networks flourish my tale has been heard by people all over the world and through sheer grit and determination it finally, after many false starts, looks to hit the big screens sometime soon. It will be another ambition fulfilled.

Since the first edition of this book all those years ago I have reached levels I could never dream about. The kid who got punched for fun became a 6th Dan Black Belt, an internationally recognised fighter and a two time Hall of Famer…not bad considering my father used to say to me "who the hell are you to do Karate?" Proved you wrong pa. But proving him wrong wasn't my goal. My goal was to find some kind of spine, a backbone bought from courage so that I may enjoy some solace. I think I succeeded. Certainly filming the trailer for the movie in a top class dojo in the States in 2013 would indicate that, especially as I was accompanied by my ever loving, ever loyal wife and children. It was a proud day indeed to share the ring with my own daughter, now a 3rd Dan Black belt herself.

So whilst my original prologue, written on a computer with a memory the size of a watch many years ago, remains here in this version, I wanted to say that today my message remains the same. No matter what your troubles, no matter how much you struggle and no matter how much you want to call it a day and give up on your dreams, don't. Don't because I know they can come true. There are many people on your path that will stand in the way and rubbish you, but there are an equal amount of people that will say "Don't give in, we can help you, we can show you how." These are the people you listen to, not the never doers. Now give 'em hell.

Simon Morrell, Fight Fortress, April 2014 (on the verge of an American Dream).

INTRODUCTION

By

Geoff Thompson BAFTA Award Winner, & Times Bestselling Author.

It is an absolute pleasure and an honour for me to write the forward to this splendid book for my very close friend Simon Morrell. A pleasure (first of all) because I love him and an honour because I am so proud of what Simon has achieved in his life.

I remember the first time I spoke to Simon on the telephone many years ago when he was still suffering with panic attacks that were managing to disable his whole life. He was so frightened at that time that even leaving the house became a war of nerves - usually the nerves winning the battle.

When I look at him now - an extremely happy, successful and brave martial arts Sixth Dan Black Belt running his own schools and fronting a successful business - it is hard to believe that this is the same timbering youth that trembled down the phone on our first conversation.

What I love about this book is not just the fact that it is extremely honest- it is and refreshingly so - rather it is the fact that the words and the author offer hope to anyone out there who is being held back by insecurity and fear. What Simon is saying is that if he can do it, if he can beat his fear and live a brave life, then so can you, so can anyone.

There is hope and there is honesty and there is inspiration in these pages that might prove lifesaving to any reader wise enough to be looking for answers and brave enough to use the information on offer.

The author of these pages is a brave man, I admire him so much that it is hard to articulate my feelings. This man not only overcame his terrifying fears of panic attacks he also - in his bid to become a better and stronger person - went on to face down a gang of drug dealers that were threatening to do unspeakable things to him and his family. He has had the courage to measure himself against the best by taking his Black Belts under some of the best Martial Artists in the world.

Simon is an ordinary man who has managed to achieve extra-ordinary things with his life and for that he should be commended. This book can offer you the inspiration to do the same.

Geoff Thompson

PROLOGUE

There is no sadder sight than that of a child walking the playground alone, having endured yet another beating, or 'mickey taking' session from cruel kids who know no better...or maybe they do. Sometimes they get a perverse kick out of the misery they cause others.

All sorts of 'reasons' are given for their behavior. Their dad didn't buy them a bike, their sister wouldn't get out of the bathroom this morning, somebody was in their seat on the bus...the list goes on.

We can talk all day and long into the night about why a bully does what he does and why a victim suffers needlessly. Sometimes the talking is justified and needed, sometimes it falls on deaf ears...the bully might just not care an ounce for his victim's pain. Hell, he might even revel in it.

But for now, back to the victim. He cares not for the bully's story. He is just sick and tired of being at the wrong end of bad behavior. Sick of getting spat at, sick of getting called hurtful, spiteful names and sick of the anxiety this problem creates.

He may even start to question his own future. Can he carry on like this? What can he do to prevent future attacks (because that is exactly what they are, attacks)? He may feel there is nothing he can do, that he is destined to a life of misery, of failure and of pain.I am happy to tell him he is wrong. There is a life beyond the suffering. There is a future with no bullies, violence or terror. Hell, it needn't be just any life either! It can be a soul-soaring, rip-roaring adventure, filled with friends, adventures, excitement and love. It can be a great life!

Trust me; I know what I am talking about. You see, I was that kid and I was that adult that endured. I wiped spit from my face, my ears burned from horrible name-calling and my body ached from the violence people cared to inflict on me. I was bullied so badly as a child and young adult that I suffered more anxiety than a man has a right to. Plagued by panic attacks I succumbed to agoraphobia. Unable to look people in the eye, people would prey on me like predators. Before I really got to grips with my problems I became the focal point for a gang of drug dealers and they too thought they could join the people who had blighted my life by bullying the very spirit out of me.

But they didn't. Nobody does anymore. They don't do that because I stopped letting them. You see I decided to take control. I was sick of the fear so I decided to take it on. It wasn't easy, it is never easy but I took control after I made the decision to do so.

It was up to me. When my chance came along and I realised I had a responsibility to myself to take that chance, I bloody well did. I took it and held onto it until it became mine, until it became me. My chance to build my self-respect came through the way of the Martial Arts but your path may be different. It really doesn't matter what path you take as long as the path fills you with confidence. As long as it builds your self-esteem so high that you feel like you are flying. In the end it isn't about fighting, it is about being.

Not everyone wants to hit the dojo floor or enter the ring but that isn't the important thing. I know people who draw their confidence from singing, painting and writing. I am lucky enough to know people from all walks of life who excel in their chosen field and exude confidence. The by-product of this is that bullies give them a wide berth because confident people will not be picked on. Life becomes a little easier to handle.

So the important thing is that you try. That you try something you really want to do but are afraid of. Maybe you are afraid of trying something because you might fail, afraid of looking silly or of being out of your depth but when you try you will find you aren't. You will find the mere fact that you are trying will lift you to a confident place and you will realise that you no longer have to be a victim.

I did it and so you can, I promise. So please, trust me, read my words and bear with me if it seems I am waffling at times. It makes sense in the end.

This book is for sufferers everywhere who are damn well sick and tired of being a victim. This book is for those people who want a good, positive way out. This is for people who have suffered and want to say 'No more! No more hiding, no more pleading. It's time I took control of my life.'

And you will.

The names of certain individuals have been changed to protect the guilty. Other than that, everything written in this book is true.

CHAPTER ONE

Things are good for me now. I have achieved lots of what I set out to achieve and I am looking forward to the challenge of achieving the ambitions I have yet to fulfil.

As I reach one goal another presents itself. In the past I would balk at such challenges, but I now know that we need challenges, fears and adversity to help us grow.

"They are tests, sent to strengthen us," a friend of mine once told me. A very wise man indeed. The tests may be of your own making, such as taking a risk in business or your personal life in order to better yourself.

It may be they are caused by the hands of another or brought about by fate. In such cases you may feel you have been dealt a bad hand and quite possibly you have. You may have been the victim of bullying or just simply another's lack of code or ethics and had to endure, what at the times, seems like endless pain and anxiety. You may feel like giving up, or more correctly you *will* feel like giving up. But if you can find the strength within yourself to last the course, see through the business risks or stand up to that bully then you may be, no, you *will* be victorious.

Sometimes the victory isn't the obvious one, and, as in my own experience, you may not even realise you have been victorious until much later, after the event. But you will do and when it hits you, the sense of confidence and well-being your victory brings will stay with you forever.

These victories will be your vehicle to, and through the next challenge. How do I know this? Because it happened to me. I have tasted both the deepest depressions and most satisfying victories.

So don't worry. You are not alone in the way you feel and there is a way forward. Many of the greatest achievers in history where prone to anxiety or started their life as victims so you are in good company. Your anxiety can be channeled into an almost unstoppable energy.

During my childhood and adolescence I was the victim of bullies. I spent my life in a dark cave of anxiety. I developed severe agoraphobia and suffered from terrifying panic attacks. At times I thought I was losing my mind. In a desperate bid to do something about it, I managed to change my life for the better. I started meeting challenges and creating opportunities for myself. However, the more opportunities I took the harder the tests where, but as a result of that, the bigger the rewards where also.

You now know that my way out of my former life as a victim was through Karate and the Martial Arts. First of all I plodded along, not daring to try and excel or stand out. But gradually I started to have some successes. People began complimenting me on my efforts and others paid me the ultimate compliment in trying to avoid fighting me. My attitude changed, not in a horrible arrogant way, but in a positive and assertive way. After training for some time I realised I had become a fighter.

Please, don't think me a coward or a bighead when I tell of my weaknesses and strengths. I tell them only to be informative, but for the first and only time in this book I apologise if what I am about to say does sound conceited.

I had become not just a fighter, but a good one at that.

However becoming good meant the tests got harder. The fights and the training where now much tougher and at times I felt like giving it all up. I wondered if it was all worth it. But the more I stuck at it the stronger I became mentally. This spilled into my life outside the combat arena and mountains suddenly became molehills. I became a much more confident, outgoing person able to contribute to all sorts of situations.

I had become a fighter on both a physical and mental level. It was a good job I did because the conflict with the drug dealer I mention in the prologue was a conflict that lasted almost three years. Imagine that? Three years of going to sleep at night worrying about the problem and waking up in the morning knowing the problem was still there. Only I could make it go away, just like only I was the only person who could put a stop to the misery of my bullying years. The funny thing was that my issue with him was nothing to do with his drugs and his dealings. It was over a legitimate business deal that went wrong.

He ripped me off over a large sum of money and then he and his gang tried to bully me into submission without paying it back. Along the way they also tried to persuade me to turn a blind eye to the dealings…right next door to my family home. Not a chance. My days at the hands of bullies where long gone, and submitting was something I no longer did. I emerged from the conflict with my hand raised. He emerged from it in the gutter where people of his ilk belong.

It took me a while to realise that I had just passed one of the biggest tests of my life and with it came the sweetest victory and its prizes.

I believe now that all my earlier misery was for a reason. People look at me like I am mad when I tell them this (can't blame them for that, I did once see a shrink!) but hopefully you will see past that initial reaction when you read this book and begin to appreciate the tests in your life. Believe me, the end results are worth it.

How did I recover from the nightmare of agoraphobia and being unable to leave the safety of my own house? How did I become someone who actually enjoys standing in front of many people, teaching them to overcome their fears and learn to defend themselves? How did I snap out of victim mode?

And perhaps the most intriguing question of all, how did I go From Bullied to Black Belt? Read on and find out, and God love you if you're a victim of any kind because you really can change the way you are. It is my extreme hope that this book will help show you how.

Here's how it all started....

"Spaz!" A mean faced kid with bright ginger hair spat the words in my face. This was the first time I was bullied. It wouldn't be the last. I was waiting in line to go into class with all the other kids. I didn't know what to do and remember feeling shocked at the hatred in his eyes. Perhaps I should have done something, answered back or been more assertive but I didn't. I did nothing. I just stood there and grinned weakly, feeling sick inside.

"Spaz!" He shouted again, to the amusement of all present. And there it was. That became my name, it became me. From then on I was then bullied into victim mode, a state that I would spend, to one degree or another, the best part of my life in.

As a youngster I always felt like an outcast and didn't seem to be able to make friends easily. Being very shy I would be an easy target for some thug to vent his frustration out on me and make a name for himself.

I can recall like it was yesterday, when I spent the day in pain after a bigger lad than me (they all seemed to be bigger lads) twisted my arm up my back until it felt like it was going to break. He only relented when I started to cry.

His idea of relenting was to push me to the ground and kick me. It was my sixth birthday. Even at that young age I was already being bullied to the degree it could have been assault.

I stumbled around the school, falling prey to both kids my own age and older. The teachers seemed no better. Once, when I didn't understand a math problem (at this age I still thought of them as sums, not math), the teacher called me to stand in front of the class. She demanded that I knew the answer. I didn't. To try and get my brain working, the teacher thought it would be a good idea to hit me across the knuckles with the sharp edge of a wooden ruler.

After dishing out her own version of inspiration, she gave me a further ten seconds to come up with the answer. Good teaching tactics these, severe pain to knuckles would help increase brain power in much the same fashion as eating a plate of fish.

Did she honestly think that the answer would suddenly spring to mind once I had felt a bit of pain? Perhaps she thought I was bluffing!

"Yeah I know the answer, you witch, but I am not going to give it to you. How many times can you hit me with your bit of wood before you get tired, eh? Believe me, I can go on forever! Your wood will break before I do!"

Sadly this wasn't the case. It just hurt. I didn't know the answer and no amount of whacking would help me produce one. After another dose of wood on knuckles I was allowed to sit down.

Humiliated and sore, I longed for a school where the teachers preferred not to beat the kids up for their inability to perform complex math at the age of seven.

I now believe that certain people can smell a victim a mile away and that these people will think nothing of adding to the misery that some of us feel. This is true of both adults and children, pupils and teachers and yes, even friends and certainly enemies. It has been my experience that if you are a weak person (but please, believe me, you can make yourself stronger) like I was, these people will exploit this for any benefit they may get, be it your dinner money or your wages at the end of the week. Yes, that's right, wages.

Bullying is not, as some may have us believe, an exclusively childhood problem. It happens on a daily basis to many adults. What may be just a laugh to the lads in work, constantly picking on one person, may to that person be a living hell. He may have to go home pretending to his wife what a great job he has and how, "The lads in work are brilliant. A right laugh!"

Deep down he may dread his working day and what it brings. It may be more than just having a laugh at someone. Violence in the workplace is now more common than ever. This little baby has spurned a whole new industry in the USA, with a multitude of books, videos and courses on how to deal with the problem, and wherever America is, we in the U.K. are never far behind.

Whether the victim of constant pranks, abuse or violence, whether male or female and whether young or old, the reasons behind your suffering don't matter to you. You just feel miserable and want it to stop.

I felt like this as early as the age of six and hated the school I was at, the people there and the kid I had become. However I persevered at this school for about four years. Only once did I attempt to stand up for myself.

A particular chap who had been using me as target practice stood with his back to me one day. A perfect chance I thought. Not very brave I admit, but for some reason I saw red and ran at him. I remember jumping on his back and pushing him to the ground. He split his head open on a concrete step and I felt I had redeemed myself.

"He deserved it," I told myself as I watched the blood gush from his head.

The head teacher thought differently and a severe reprimand followed then I was beaten with a cane. The bully got a cold drink and an afternoon off school. This took the wind out of my sales. I now didn't know if it was right to fight back as all

I got was into trouble. I went immediately back into a depression and fell victim to the bullies again.

Sleepless nights and dreadful mornings followed. I took the decision to approach my Dad and asked to change schools. I missed the school bus deliberately and instead went to my Dad's office.

"I was in the shop, Dad, and the bus must have been early," I offered by way of explanation.

"Well I'll take you in, come on, get in the car," he said, moving to get up from behind his desk.

I decided it was time for him to know the truth. Tears filled my eyes and in one breath I poured out to him the miserable time I had been having for the last few years.

He listened and then asked me what I wanted to do. It was simple. I wanted to change schools.

"Okay, I'll phone the school now and tell them you won't be going back," he promised. I was sent to get some sweets and a drink whilst he made the phone call. He was in mid-conversation when I returned. Pausing he put his hand over the mouthpiece.

"Your head teacher has promised that if you go back, he will personally see to it that you aren't bullied anymore," he offered.

Panic set in. "No, no, I just don't want to go back there, please!"

I had no faith whatsoever in the head, his teachers or his school. The very thought of returning filled me with fear.

"Okay, that's fine. You don't have to go back if you don't want to."

My Dad turned back to the phone and gave the headmaster the good news. My escape had been arranged all the way to the border. I wouldn't be returning to junior Colditz. Instead I was transferred to a different school, away from my tormentors.

It was with a smile on my face and a spring in my step that I entered my new school. I had a fresh start where nobody knew me. The children seemed okay and I was put in the protective custody of two girls, Josie and Debbie.

As I was the new lad, I was something of a novelty and it was at this school, once Josie and Debbie had become bored with me and let me off the leash, that I made my first proper best friend.

Richard was the same age as me and we both shared a passion for sports and in particular Liverpool Football Club and their star player, Kevin Keegan. Richard and I played for hours, swapping places at pretending to be Keegan and for what seemed like the first time, I enjoyed school.

However, things were short lived. We had a fall out, as ten year olds do and fisticuffs were arranged. You would think by now that I had realised that I couldn't fight my way out of a wet paper bag.

But no, my thinking was that this was different. I wasn't being bullied (and in this case I wasn't), but this was a proper fight of which I was a willing participant. I was ready for it.

When we did get around to fighting, Richard absolutely hammered me (well in the way that ten year olds do) but he was such a nice lad that he cried more than me and reported himself to the teacher!

Holding us both by the hand, the teacher didn't have the heart to tell us off but got an agreement from us that fighting was pointless. We went back to being friends and I thought that was the end of my trips out into violence.

However, having seen what a useless pugilist I was became the inspiration for another kid, Timmy, to try and make my head and the toilet wall one and the same thing. Very big for his age, and strong with it, Timmy approached me in the toilets. Without warning he grabbed my hair and smashed my head into a concrete wall. I was shocked, by both the speed and surprise of the attack. No words were spoken, just actions taken and I was left dazed, in a hump on the floor.

Somebody told the teacher of my distress, which led to a very strange series of events. Timmy was called to stand in front of the class, whilst I sat nervously in my chair. The teacher addressed the class on the wrongfulness of trying to 'amalgamate somebody's head with a wall'. We looked on blankly…we didn't know what amalgamate meant as we were only ten years old.

Then she did something that totally surprised us.

"Simon, would you like to come up here and smash Timmy's head into the wall?" she asked.

I couldn't believe it. The teachers in this school were great! Somebody shouted an encouraging "Yeah!" and so, to the cheers of my classmates, I left my chair and made my way to the front. Timmy watched, horrified, as I approached but when I got there, the teacher's attitude changed.

"Simon don't you dare, I am disgusted with you!" she yelled. "Sit down now!"

Slightly confused at this withdrawal of invitation, I went back to my seat. Timmy was also told to sit down and the class resumed its work. I looked around at the kids with their heads buried in their books and wondered if I had just imagined the whole thing. Not one of the kids ever mentioned it again but at least Timmy just left me alone.

As time passed, High School loomed on the horizon and with it the prospect of even bigger kids and tougher bullies. I had now become very shy, even skinnier and confidence was something I could not even entertain. I was rubbish at sport and not particularly bright and so tried to keep a low profile in a school of sixteen hundred kids.

The problem was I could keep a low profile to most, but not to all. At the age of about fourteen, I was out one day riding my bike, minding my own business.

A local thug, RW, took offence to this for some unknown reason. He thought he was hilarious and a charmer but I had seen this kid in school and knew him to be nasty piece of work. Until now, I hadn't had the pleasure of meeting him in person but that was about to change. As I rode past him, to the amusement of his friends, he ran at me and grabbed hold of the front of my bike.

"Give me my fucking bike!" he screamed.

"It isn't yours," I argued meekly as I desperately tried to hold onto it.

"Well what about the smokes you owe me!" he yelled into my face.

"I don't owe you any," I tried to argue.

"You fucking do! Bring them here tomorrow or you're dead!"

With a parting slap around my head he was gone. The feeling of sickness is something I will remember forever. Panic, stomach churning, light-headedness and I didn't even smoke!

I spent a restless night worrying about the next day's events and what I would do. I decided I would ignore the whole thing thinking it would go away and for a while I lived in ignorant bliss. However, a change of fortune would bring RW back into my life.

I had a trial for the local football team and made the position as goalkeeper. The qualification for this was that I was the only one who could be bothered to try out for it. It was the first time I felt I had actually achieved something and looked forward to being part of a team. The team's pitch was at the bottom of the road into a large housing estate, which happened to be the haunt of RW.

To get to the pitch I had to enter the estate at the very corner where RW was to be found hanging around. The alternative was to cycle two miles out of my way to enter the training area via the local rubbish dump... I chose the rubbish dump route. The extra two miles I had to cycle were great for my fitness but by God, the rubbish smelt!

I was picked to play for my first game against a local team. Instead of being overjoyed, I was terrified. You see a "friend" had taken pleasure in informing me that RW would often be seen at the matches, hurling abuse at the players. So instead of looking forward to the match, I spent all of the day before, a Friday, shaking and feeling physically sick.

Some of the kids noticed how ill I looked and asked if I was okay, yet not one adult, teacher or otherwise, even noticed that I was pale and could not stop shaking.

However, it turned out my fear was all just a waste of energy. RW was nowhere to be seen. I scanned the area constantly whilst we waited for the cars to pick us up and take us to the opposition's ground. It was with a sigh of relief that I got into my Dad's car and relaxed as he drove us to our match. So all that worrying was for nothing!

I could now just concentrate on the game and my opportunity to become a hero by saving everything that the opposition threw at me. Surely, this was my time!

It wasn't. We lost sixteen to one. As if I didn't have enough baggage, my newfound "friends and team mates" hated me as well. I had to put up with comments like, "You couldn't save at a supermarket!" as I walked through the school.

I persevered only because I felt too ashamed to quit. After a couple of months on a dark cold night, I decided to take a chance and make my way home through the estate. It had been ages since I had seen RW and I was too tired to take the long way home.

It was a bad move! As I approached the corner where RW and his cronies hung out, I noticed a figure running toward me. Terrified, with panic rushing through me, I tried to pedal faster but I had no chance. RW was too fast and too strong for me. He grabbed hold of my handlebars and jumped on my bike's front wheels, stopping me in my tracks.

"I have fucking told you, where's my fags!" Surely a question, not an instruction (no, I wasn't that smart and didn't say that to him at the time).

"I forgot, I'm sorry!" I stuttered. His smack around my head made sure I would not forget again. For just a minute, it looked like I might have a reprieve.

"Leave him alone Ricky!" one of his mates laughed.

"Shut up, he owes me fags!" Ricky screamed back at him.

"I am sorry, I'll bring them tomorrow honest!" I pleaded.

"You better do, now get lost!"

I did not need telling twice, I was off like a shot. Another sleepless night followed and I made the decision to get him the cigarettes. This brought another problem. I had to find some money. I had some savings in the building society and managed to smuggle my savings book out of the house. I withdrew the minimum allowed, five pounds, and made my way to the local shop then, for the first time in my life, bought a packet of cigarettes.

Armed with the goods, I made my way to the park to meet Ricky. I waited nervously for what seemed like an age. He never showed up. Is that bad mannered or what? Even he didn't realise what a weak character I was, he just didn't think I would buy him cigarettes, but as I waited, a lad I vaguely knew from school wandered by.

"What are you doing here, Morrell?" he asked.

I explained my position and he laughed.

"Forget it, if you give into him now he will just keep getting stuff off you"

I sat on a swing looking down, knowing what he said was true.

"What will I do?" I asked, "I can't fight him."

"Then tell your Mum and Dad."

I nodded. They would tell me off for taking money from my account but it would be worth it. I approached my Mum first, when my Dad was out having a drink. She was horrified. She sat down for a think. My Dad had a friend who was a policeman and she rang him for advice. After a while he phoned back to speak to me.

"He won't bother you anymore Simon, a friend has had a word and he will leave you alone," he told me. A feeling of shame dampened my relief.

"What a coward I am," I told myself. "Still, at least I'm free from him now".

However, my freedom was short lived. My first girlfriend brought with her a psycho that made RW look like a family friend.

CHAPTER TWO

Maria was lovely. A popular girl in a different class but in the same year as me. I admired her from afar until somebody noticed my interest. Of course, they had to let her know. At first she just laughed, but then amazingly, she considered my request. A date with me! I took my chance as I was usually too shy for this kind of thing but late one Tuesday night I found myself at her front door.

"Everyone has been saying you will go out with me. Is it true?" I asked, hopefully.

She nodded, "Yes alright."

So a date was set up and the following night I waited outside the cinema for her. She turned up late, possibly an omen of what horrors the next year would bring. I still remember the film was 'The Blues Brothers' but I saw nothing of it. I spent the whole time wondering if I was supposed to kiss her goodnight. The walk home was awkward and when we stopped at the bottom of my road to say goodnight, I just couldn't pluck up the courage to try and kiss her. What was worse, I realised that she had walked me home, not me her!

For reasons only Maria knew, she agreed to see me again (she must of done a lot for charity) and I was over the moon. Next time I would kiss her, for definite!

However, things were to go from good to incredibly frightening, very quickly. Some days later I was walking home from a friend's house on a summer Sunday afternoon when two youths approached me.

"Are you Simon Morrell?" the tough looking one asked.

"Yes," I replied, unsure of why he wanted to know.

"Oh," he continued. "Don't you go out with Maria?"

"Oh yes," I beamed with pride thinking he was paying me a compliment. He wasn't...Bang! Out of nowhere he threw a punch into my face that slammed me against the wall. Then I was gripped by the collar.

"You stay away from her right! She's mine!" he ordered. Don't bullies have a way with words?

"I'm sorry, I didn't know, honest," came my shaky reply. His friend seemed shocked at the violence.

"Leave it Jimmy, he didn't know," he shouted.

Jimmy just glared at me with coal black eyes.

"I'm a lot stronger than you, Morrell!" he spat. But funnily enough, I could feel that he wasn't. I knew deep down I could have just pushed him off. I just didn't have the courage to try it. Instead, I just became the same bullied kid I was when I was four years old and answered with a weak nod, feeling sick and ashamed inside. He let me go and I scuttled home, humiliated. When would this bullying that had followed me around all my life stop? I know now that it would stop as soon as I stopped allowing it to happen. I just didn't know this at the time.

Maria however, had her own version of their romance.

"We finished ages ago, he just won't accept it. He's a head case you know." My God, this girl was perceptive! "He's just been up in court for stabbing someone with a screwdriver, " she continued. "Do you know that long coat he wears?"

I nodded, anxious to hear about more of Jimmy's talents.

"Well in the inside pockets, he keeps a knife as well!"

Jesus, this just gets better and better! I thought long and hard about it and decided that if Maria would still go out with me, then I would go out with her, and suffer the consequences!

Easier said the done. One night, I was sitting in our kitchen having a cup of tea when the doorbell rang.

"Si, your friends are here for you," my Mum said.

I went to the door to see who it was. Standing there, grinning like a big grinning thing and looking like the main character from a murder movie was Jimmy.

"Fancy a game of football?" he asked with a wicked grin on his face. I was shocked! Behind him, stood a mutual friend, Mike, desperately shaking his head, trying to let me know not to come outside. Like I needed telling.

"No thanks," I stuttered to Jimmy.

"Let me ask you, how many times have you been with Maria this week? I don't mean sexually, I mean just you and her, out alone." His question shocked me. Sexually?! Christ, I hadn't even kissed her yet!

"Look, I don't know what you want. My Mum and Dad are here, leave me alone"

"So? Big deal your dad is here. So what?" He didn't seem impressed by this information.

"I've got to go," I said as I shut the door.

He grinned at me through the porch window.

"Five minutes!" he shouted; an order, not a request.

But I didn't. goThe next day I bumped into Mike.

"I'm sorry Simon. He threatened to batter me if I didn't take him to your house," he explained.

"It's alright, it's not your fault. He's a head case."

I didn't blame Mike. However, here, unbeknown to me, came my first 'gift of fear'. The gift of awareness. I didn't realise it at the time, but my survival instincts made me become very switched on, very quickly. In my effort to avoid Jimmy and further threats and violence, I spent every day scanning the school grounds for the threat he would carry. I would scrutinize every nook and cranny for a sight of his ugly mug.

This raised my awareness levels and this is something I would, much later on in life, come to rely on heavily to protect myself, and more importantly my wife and children, from a very volatile situation. It also forms a big part of my Self Protection teachings, so,, as I said earlier, there are gifts everywhere; it's just that sometimes we don't realise it until much later.

For now though, avoiding Jimmy was enough. I managed to stay out of his way for a couple of months but being in a small town high school, bumping into him was inevitable, whether I was developing awareness or not.

Walking back to school one lunchtime, I heard his voice shout to me:

"Simon!" I turned to him, terrified.

"You alright mate?" he asked gently, in a way that a friend would.

"Yeah, I'm great!" I responded. I was completely taken aback by his pleasant attitude and seeming change of mind about me. I was also relieved that he was being nice.

"Good," he nodded.

I was so happy, light with relief. I don't know what had happened to bring this sudden change of events, but who cared? I was free again. I dropped my awareness like a hot brick which would prove to be a big mistake.

A few days later I was walking through the school and as I turned the corner I came face to face with him. I still felt a tingle of adrenaline despite the fact that there was now, supposedly, a truce. Well not so much as a truce, rather he had apparently become bored with stalking me but there was to be no such luck. Whatever charity he had been feeling the other day was replaced with the usual viciousness. A short punch to my stomach and the wind shot out of me. I felt sick again. Jimmy just carried on walking as if nothing had happened, leaving me in a state of anxiousness, not for the first or indeed the last time in my life.

As winter set in, it seemed it was going to be a long one, with me frightened to go out of the house, and when I did I would be constantly scanning and avoiding. I had learnt my lesson in this sense, and I would not be dropping my guard again.

I felt safe inside our home and spent most of my time listening to records, the soundtracks from Quadrophenia and

The Wanderers keeping me company. However, this sanctuary was soon to be violated. One night, whilst my Dad was out playing snooker we had a phone call from a neighbor. She informed my Mum that there was a large gang gathering outside our house.

Sure enough, when we looked out of the window we saw Jimmy, surrounded by a group of lads all waiting to see the lamb brought to slaughter.

"Who are they?" my Mum asked me. I couldn't answer. I was shocked into silence. "I'm calling the police," she told me.

Not again! I was so scared and embarrassed by my lack of courage. I managed to persuade her to wait for a while. It can't have been easy for her, she must have been frightened with all these hooligans sat in her front garden. Thankfully, after what seemed like an age, they left. My relief at them going, I would come to realise, was going to be short lived.

The next day at school, I was told that he was planning another home visit for that night. Upon hearing this I did something that both surprised me and frightened me. I decided to fight him.

"No more!" I thought "I've got to do something. I would rather get battered than keep on going like this." I made my mind up to fight him and be done with it, one way or another. Suddenly, with this decision, I felt better than I had for a long time. Certainly I was still frightened, but the feelings were a lot less intensive now that I had come to terms with what had to be done. I started to turn my feelings of fear into feelings of anger. And so, on yet another dark and windy night, I found myself in the company of my sister and my best friend, both of whom were there to offer encouragement, as I waited to do battle with the scariest person I had ever met.

We sat in the kitchen, waiting for the doorbell to ring, with our nerves jangling. The plan was, when the time came, for me to open the door and just hit him. I really believed I could do it.

Either way I was sick of the whole episode, and sick of waiting for him to turn up.

It was a long, long night. Every bang and bump that the wind produced, the gate banging or the windows rattling, bought with it another surge of adrenaline.

We waited. And waited. And waited. All for nothing. He didn't show. I have no idea, even to this day, why. I was both relieved and strangely disappointed but still felt very wound up.

I then did something that was unforgivable. In a silly argument brought on by the tension, I punched my friend in the mouth. My sister was horrified and my friend looked hurt (his feelings, not his mouth) as I sloped off to bed, ashamed. He was a good friend and had chosen to stay with me that night when he could of been in a hundred different places. I chose to hit him instead of thank him.

I realise now, years later and after much soul searching and training, that my actions were just my body needing a release from the stress. I know now that, if I have had a conflict or row with no physical release (and not getting "physical" is by far the better option) then I need to find a surrogate release.

Now I am not the kind of person who likes to kick my dogs (a good job given the fact that they are two rather large German Shepherds!) so I will release my stress by training. This may take the form of punching the bag, weight training, or grappling and sparring with a willing training partner. This not only helps keep me fit, develops technique and character and hones up my Self Protection skills, but it burns up any adrenaline I may have rushing around my body. If I don't do this, I may get a little depressed and I will feel wound up and angry, taking it out on someone who doesn't deserve it.

This is what happened on the night in question. My mum and dad grounded me for two weeks, my sister didn't speak to me and worst of all, once I woke in the morning, I found all my courage had left me. I wouldn't fight Jimmy as my bravery had disappeared. I felt sick again. My brief trip into 'Warriorship' was replaced by the ever-corroding fear that was brought to yet another level one bright summer's evening.

I had avoided Jimmy for some time, and tried to ignore the delight in people's voices as they sought me out to give me the good news.

"He's still looking for you."

Avoidance couldn't last forever, and inevitably our paths crossed again. By this time Maria had long finished with me and moved onto another boyfriend, but Jimmy had latched onto my victim mode and made it his own.

I was walking up the local high street with a couple of pals when a voice shouted out to me from behind:

"Simon, come here!"

I turned and was rooted to the spot at the sight of the shaven headed Jimmy, practically frothing at the mouth. I couldn't move with the fear as he walked toward me. Luckily, a girl from our school ran past Jimmy and broke my daze. Her exact words will stay with me forever.

"Simon, he's got a knife! Run!" she screamed, terrified.

Jimmy ran at me brandishing his blade. I needed no further encouragement and turned on my heels, terrified. I sprinted about half a mile to a friend's house and banged on the door, on the verge of hysteria. Jimmy was just steps behind me waving his blade, intent written all over his face.

My friend's mum opened the door and I pushed past her into the house. She tried to calm me down as I listened to the row outside. My shame grew as I realised that my two friends were having a go back at Jimmy. One was attempting to bash Jimmy in the head with a large stick whilst the other was shouting at him to, "Just leave Simon alone!"

Jimmy lost interest quickly at this sudden, unexpected turn of events, and, walking into the sunset and out of harm's way, turned and pointed at my friends, knife now back in its hiding place:

"You are both dead, and Morrell's too!"

It's funny, later on in life, when, after a lot of tough training and real life confrontations and when I was able to handle conflicts much better, I came to realise that most people threaten you as they walk away. They will tell you they are going to attack you or do you harm, whilst putting as much distance between you and them as possible. These limited people usually share the same lines such as:

"I'll be back for you!" Or the old favorite "Don't walk down any dark alleys, you won't know when it's coming but it's fucking coming!"

I once had somebody, backed by a six strong gang, inform me, "I'll have my day with you, not today, but soon!"

When I pointed out the almost overwhelming odds in his favor and that he may not actually get a better day than this and that he should surely seize his chance now, but warning him that if he did I would "batter the life out of him!" he seemed to go off the idea.

"No," I could see his little brain working overtime, as he thought to himself, "I'm sure there will be a better chance. Next time I might have even more back up! I'll leave it for now and go back home to take more drugs. Yes, that will be best."

And with that he turned on his heels and, along with his merry men, walked in the other direction to that in which I felt an attack might actually take place (more on this incident later).

You see, I feel that for someone to attack you they must be at least reasonably close to you, so a movement of 'towards' must be adopted, not 'away'. In other words, most bullies are full of shit. But you have to be careful. Some aren't, and if your bluff is called, you had better be prepared and capable of backing your words up.

However, at the time of the incident with Jimmy and his knife, I was not equipped with this knowledge, just frightened for my life. Once Jimmy had been gone for some time, I made plans to go home. I could have walked along the main road, a direct route and only about ten minutes to my house. However, there would be chance that Jimmy might be around and I just couldn't risk it. Instead, I took the path of least resistance, depending on your point of view. I went the long way around, which involved hiking up some very steep hills, walking back on my tracks along a disused railway line and cutting through our back hedge into our garden, a trip of about half an hour. For company, I had my shame. I had to do something about this, but didn't know what.

Two days later, back at school, I was sitting in my technical drawing class, getting on with my work. The teacher had gone to have one of his regular cigarettes (Woodbines) hence his nickname, 'Woody'. I sat in a group of four. One of the four was a chap called Gary. Now Gary wasn't a bad sort by any means, but he did like to walk around with his chest puffed out 'John Wayne' style and loved to tell you about his rugby battles.

He generally regarded himself as a hard lad and was part of the school's "hard lad's club". He wasn't exactly a bully, but could be pushed that way if he wanted to be.

I sat quietly at my desk discovering all kinds of wonderful things about right angles, rulers and compasses whilst most of the class was in mayhem, throwing things at each other. Who should wander in but Jimmy? I nearly died. I slid behind my drawing board trying to become invisible, the by now regular panic setting in. Gary noticed my discomfort and picked up on it. He turned to Jimmy and shouted, "Hey Jim! Over here!" then turned to me and grinned, slyly.

"Please don't Gary, please, he'll kill me!"
"I know" he laughed. "Jimmy, here, look who's over here!"

Jimmy hadn't heard him yet, he was busy talking to someone else so Gary persisted:

"Jimmy, look who's hiding from you!"

"Shut up Gary!" ordered a girl sitting with us. It was my Guardian Angel again, the girl who had opened my eyes to the knife last time Jimmy and I had met.

"Yeah Gary, just leave him," another kid added.

Gary sat there, laughing at me, oblivious to the terror his actions where inflicting. I remember him raising his eyebrows and grinning. I looked down embarrassed. He did shut up but he had enjoyed every minute of it, whilst I hated him to pieces for his cruelty. He had no need to be spiteful in an already bad situation.

But there is a good twist to this tale. Many years later, I crossed paths with Gary again. I reminded him of the incident but he laughed and claimed not to remember it. Both of us knew he did, however we did become good friends.

I had at the time been teaching Martial Arts for some time, and Gary expressed an interest in joining my class. I was happy to take him in. I suppose I still considered the roles we both assumed when we were kids and thought him to be the tough guy whilst I was the weaker of us, but complete role reversal took place on this one. Here, I was the one completely at home on the mats, and, whilst Gary had a fair talent, I dominated every match we had. He was unable to match me for speed, power, fitness or strength. A complete contrast to our earlier days, as bully and bullied. He trained for quite some time and reached a decent level, when it all came crashing in for him.

I was training for a Full Contact Fight at one of Europe's toughest clubs. Gary had promised to be my sparring partner leading up to it. Several heavy sessions had passed by when Gary suggested "Let's pick it up a bit." I don't think he meant to sound clever, but genuinely wanted to help me by putting more pressure on. We touched gloves and his fifteen stone frame moved menacingly toward my nine and a half. He started trying to land big heavy shots, which I avoided or swatted away with the inside of my glove.

A couple of double jabs had him on his back feet, and a couple of body shots slowed him down a bit. About halfway through the second round (we had set ourselves six) I could see him set himself. He planted his feet, and with his gloves held high around his head, he pulled slightly back with his right hand, ready to throw a big one. He left a very small gap between guard and face. I remember thinking, in the split second beforehand, "I'm having that!" and threw a short left uppercut that made it through the gap in between his gloves and caught him just under the nose. He dropped like a sack of potatoes, blood gushing everywhere. Stunned, he just didn't know where he was. He later told me that the doctor had informed him I had split the membrane between his mouth and nose. He never trained again.

We brought him round and looked after him, giving him plenty of water and cleaning him up. It was several weeks before his voice returned to normal. I found it ironic and a little bit weird that I could hit people like this and do this kind of damage especially lads much bigger than me.

I suppose I still hadn't come to terms with all the training I had done. I also found it "unusual" to have done it to one of my former bullies.

However, after the situation in the technical drawing room, weeks passed without further incident. Then, whilst out with my sister one sunny afternoon I spotted Jimmy on the local field. I ran past the field to safety behind a wall.

Up to this point my sister hadn't seen Jimmy in the flesh, only heard about him. She looked confused at my sudden run until I explained who I had seen.

"Right, leave this to me!" she ordered.

This couldn't get any worse. Now my sister was fighting my battles for me. She stormed toward the pitch with good intentions, but I think once she was there she ran out of ideas so just stood staring at him until he caught sight of her.

"What are you looking at?!" he screamed at her.

"You, that's who!" Jackie shouted back.

"Yeah, well you fuck off, you slag!" he replied. He must have been up all night thinking of that one. She glared at him in a last effort to frighten him and then made her way to where I was hiding.

"Well, how did it go?" I asked.

She looked at me, worried. "Christ he's a baddie isn't he?"

"Shit…" was all I could manage to say.

CHAPTER THREE

Something then happened that, unquestionably, changed my life for the better. It took a long time to change and longer for me to realise it had indeed changed, but change for the better it did.

The change came when I was introduced to Karate. My sister, in an effort to help me beat my bullies, claimed she had seen an advert in a shop for a local school and suggested that we both give it a try. We both gave it some thought but no more was said about it until Jackie went out on a date with a man who had met her when he went into the factory where she worked to get his punch bag fixed.

It turned out that the guy was a Black Belt at Karate. Jackie hadn't seen any advert after all, it was just a story to try and get me to try it. Sean suggested that she should try to get me to start training.

"Why don't you give it a go?" she suggested, "I'll start with you."

And so it was, on that one summer evening, I started my journey in the Martial Arts. It is a journey I am still on, some thirty three years later, and one that would take me to places I never dreamt I would go, to become friends with my heroes, people I never imagined I ever would meet, let alone share a bond with. It would also be a journey that would see me achieve dreams that I thought were well beyond anything I was capable of. It would be a path that would, on more than one occasion and in more than one form, save my life.

However, on my first night I found myself nervously shuffling into a church hall filled with people who had forgotten to change from their nightwear that morning, still in their shiny white pajamas. My sister's new boyfriend approached me.

"Do you want to join in or watch?" he asked kindly.

"I'll join in," I said, surprising myself at my lack of shyness and some courage.

The style was the very traditional and very strong art of Shotokan Karate, and to me, some of the lads training there where awesome. I was hooked, and from that moment I knew I wanted to be, and would become, a Black Belt. Through mishaps and setbacks, some admittedly self engineered others the result of the cruel fate I mentioned in the introduction, it would take me almost fifteen years to get it. It takes the average student about five.

Either way, that day in the church hall showed me a way out of being bullied. It was up to me to take the chance and take it I did. I started training as often as I could. I knew though, that after only a couple of week's training I was still no match for Jimmy.

Punching the air in the gym and visualizing his face made me feel wonderful. Yet I would still crash back down to earth whenever there was a chance I would see him, and I was about to see meet him again very soon:

As chance or fate would decree, I had been asked to play in a football match. The pitch adjoined the youth centre that Jimmy went to. I was reluctant to play there and tried to get the lads to change the venue but they wouldn't. The match had already been arranged so I was either in or out and seeing how invitations weren't exactly piling up, I chose in.

I stood in the goalmouth (yep, they put me in goal again!), watching anxiously for any sight of him. Every person that appeared at the pitch sent my heart into fear fuelled palpitations.

About half and hour into the game I heard a blood curling scream. Looking up I saw Jimmy on the back of his mate's bike, followed by his gang of cronies. My legs turned to Jelly as he cast his glare over me.

"Morrell, you bastard, you're dead after this!" he screamed.

He then did something that frightened the life out of me. He climbed up a tree, and sat on a branch staring at me and making noises like a monkey.

I should have realised two things. One, the monkey thing was just an act to get me to run away. Two, if he was really going to get me as he said he was, then he would have done it straight away. After all, what was stopping him? Was he worried about getting the referee's red card?

However, at the time I didn't realize. I took off sprinting across the pitch to the safety of nearby houses. I am ashamed to say I left my little brother at the side of the pitch as I scrambled over a garden wall to safety. I banged on the hysterically first door I came to. Here I was again. Same shit, different day.

An elderly gentleman opened the door and I blurted out to him:

"Please, I've got no money but I've got to use your phone. I need my dad! There are some lads that are going to kill me! My little brother is still there!"

He looked confused but let me in and handed me the phone. I could feel my bowels swishing with adrenalin and fear as I waited for my Dad to come to the phone. When he did he listened as I let it all out and he promised to be there in seconds.

I put the phone down and stalled for time in the safety of this stranger's house. He wasn't impressed. "Don't you think you better go and see if your brother is alright?" he admonished.

"Yes, I will," I conceded reluctantly. I made my way back to the pitch a lot slower than I left it. To my relief, my Dad and his mate where already there.

"What's going on Si?" my dad ask

This was the first my dad knew of any of this. I gave him a brief history, leaving out the more serious issue of the attempted stabbing in case I got caught up in a police situation.

My dad turned to Jimmy. With everyone watching it quickly became a classical 'Mexican Standoff'. "If you go near my son again, I will break your legs with a baseball bat right!" he barked.

Jimmy glared at my dad with his chilling, coal black eyes. "When he's eighteen," he replied, calmly.

"What?" my dad asked, obviously confused by this cocky little thug in front of him.

"When's he's eighteen and out of your control, I am going to kill him".

The atmosphere was like ice and I thought I was going to throw up. "I don't care if he is eighteen, twenty eight or whatever. He is my son now stay away from him, I'm warning you!" barked my dad.

"When he's eighteen" Jimmy repeated, very calmly.

"Yeah, you try it!" my dad countered.

The horrible stand off continued, neither of them giving ground. It was quiet for what seemed like hours as they just stood staring at each other, the crowd waiting to see who blinked first...it was my dad.

"Get in the car Simon. I'm taking you home!" he ordered.

Jimmy couldn't help but award himself a victory smirk as we got into the car and drove home. I went straight to my room and my dad went with his friend for a beer. Sitting on my bed, I discussed this latest episode and its possible backlashes with a friend who had joined us.

"Well, if he is going to do it when I am eighteen, he should watch it. I'll have put on weight and will be a least a purple and white belt at karate by then!"

Naively, I had worked it all out. My friend said nothing, possibly knowing my words were a fantasy.

Later that evening, my dad came to give me a talk. He told me I would have to start standing up for myself, stop letting anyone and everyone push me around. I knew what he said was true but I just didn't know how to deal with it. I always felt so afraid. Nobody else seemed scared, so there must have been something wrong with me. There wasn't. I just didn't know it then. Years later, I realised that everybody is afraid to some degree. Some just hide it better than others. It is all right to be scared. It is how you deal with this fear that separates you from the rest.

When I was able to accept this, I was able to turn tables on it, and when situations demanded, I was able to make the opposition beat themselves by their own fear. You too can do this, whatever your fears are. You just have to know how, or be willing to learn how, and then take that knowledge and put it to the test.

However, none of this applied to me on this summer night as I settled down in bed, ashamed in the knowledge that my dad now knew what I, and many others, had known for a long time…his son was a coward.

Surprisingly, Jimmy left me alone after that, but not after one last attempt to finish me off. A friend of his, who as there on the night of the football match, was sent to find me.

"Jimmy is still going to get you. He couldn't give a shit what your dad said. He says he's going to hurt you. You have to be really, really careful here, Si, " my friend informed me.

I shrugged. What could I do? I was tired of the whole thing. But he never did. Jimmy never came for me again and I didn't see him again until some years later. I don't know where he had been and I didn't care. When I saw him again it was in a nightclub. He sat opposite me and I felt the all too familiar tingle of fear. This was before my "no more victim days", before I had developed Fighting Spirit when I was still scared of my own shadow. I was worried he would recognise me and felt like running from the club. It seemed like some things never change.

After a couple of minutes he turned and saw me, his stone black eyes catching mine. Panic started to take hold of me but he just nodded to me and went back to drinking his pint. Relief flooded through me. Ten minutes later, he was at the bar when a fight broke out. Amazingly, Jimmy tried to stop it. The bouncers came charging through the door and one of them eclipsed Jimmy with a huge punch and then dragged him out and threw him down the stairs.

I don't know, maybe it is not even my place to say, but was it karma or "just desserts"? He hadn't done anything wrong but suffered anyway, at the hands of another. It reminded me of someone else who had been an innocent victim, in the wrong place at the wrong time.

Five minutes later, Jimmy returned. The barmaid had, quite correctly, informed the doormen of Jimmy's peacekeeping attempts. They dusted him off, bought him a drink and he wore his wounds like a medal for all to see. More importantly for me at that time, he did not bother me that night.

After this incident, many years would pass before I next saw him again. We were both different then. I had been training for many years and was by now, quite a capable fighter. I had come to terms with certain fears and was no longer the bullied kid I had been all those years ago.

Incredibly, Jimmy and I stopped to have a chat with each other. "I have been told I was terrible to you when we were younger?" he asked. A mutual friend had recently reminded him of our past history.

"Yeah you were," I laughed. He bothered me no more, I towered above him in both stature and, I believed, ability.

"I'm sorry," he continued. "I did a lot of bad things back then that I don't even remember now. I took all sorts of substances. I did a lot of bad stuff." He looked me in the eye when he said it. It didn't really matter, it had been a terrible time, but it had helped, in a funny way, to form me.

"Forget it. It was a long time ago," I replied.

We shook hands, and I think, we kind of acknowledged that any 'conflict' between us would now have a completely different result. I would not be the one running or cowering in the corner. Those days where long gone.

CHAPTER FOUR

If "siege by Jimmy" had almost completely demoralised me, then my Karate was, for what seemed the first time, giving me a bit of hope.

I had started training a couple of times a week, diligently marching up and down the training hall, throwing kicks and punches and shouting "Kias!" (a shout to show spirit). It seemed to be doing me good. I was still only about fifteen years old, and had been training for just a couple of months, when I was approached outside the high school one afternoon, by a group of lads set on having a laugh at my expense. They berated me and I could see they looked on me as a bit of fun to be pushed around.

"Dear me," I chuckled to myself, "Didn't these guys know I did Karate?!"

I wanted to see if the Karate I was being taught worked. Of course it worked. The reality was however, that I didn't know, after such a naively short training period, how to make it do so.

As I stood in front of them, preparing to 'teach them a lesson' I made a long Karate stance, left arm in front, right hand pulled back to the side in a fist. I then launched the slowest "step and punch" ever. It was the only technique I could remember, but it took such a long time to reach my opponent that he had time to sit down, do his homework and eat an apple. He then he got up and battered me!

He smashed me to the floor, jumped on top of me, hit me a couple of times and asked me had I had enough. I had and nodded my submission.

He laughed in my face and rolled off me, walking away with his mates. Some guys who had been watching looked at me and shook their heads in both amusement and disgust.

I turned to my two friends for some support or comfort. They just shrugged their shoulders as if my beating was a given. The three of us carried on walking back to my house for lunch.

I decided to carry on training, despite it seemingly failing me. I explained to my instructor, Sean, Jackie's boyfriend, what had happened. I told him that once I was on the floor, I couldn't get my opponent off.

In all fairness, he tried to work out a couple of moves in answer to the problem, but they were very ineffective and about four days to late. It wasn't entirely his fault. The style we were practicing didn't cover ground defense at all. It was only many years later when I was introduced to wrestling, grappling and floor fighting, and having had the benefit of some excellent teachers, that I realised how difficult, but how important, groundwork is. For now though, I would have to hope that I was beaten up vertically and not horizontally.

Despite this latest beating, as the summer moved on my training progressed and I was asked if I wanted to enter a competition. I was pleased at being asked, and though I was nervous to the point of being sick, I awoke on the Sunday morning of the competition, determined to have a go.

I imagined the tournament, which was to be held at Liverpool University, would be a rather low-key affair. I have no idea what made me think that as I could not have been more wrong.

Dubbed "The North of England Championships" and hosted by one of the world's most respected organisations, 'The Karate Union of Great Britain', it attracted people from all over the country. There were that many people queuing to get in, I thought there had been an accident and people were stopping to watch.

After we warmed up and it got nearer my time to fight, I felt the old sickness of fear coming back and panic starting to take hold. Some of the team rallied around, and as always, my sister was there to offer encouragement. I soon put my mind to the fighting about to take place and tried to forget about my worries.

There were about eight fighting areas and I was assigned to one. I had no idea what to do when they called my name. No one had told me what to expect or how to respond. I just stood in the crowd like a lemon.

In the area itself was a Karate-ka standing in the ready stance, wearing a Black Belt, so with me only being a white belt I felt some mistake had been made. No, there had been no mistake and they called my name again. One of our instructors pushed me forward onto the fighting area.

"When you're called, you come okay!" the referee admonished.

I nodded that I understood and then he said something in Japanese. When he did, Black Belt responded by moving forward and hitting me! The referee raised his arm in the Black Belt's direction and he was awarded a point.

He had hit me in the nose and my eyes streamed with water. I was vaguely aware that someone in the crowd laughed and shouted, "He's crying!"

"I'm bloody not!" I wanted to shout, but I knew this wouldn't go down well. Instead, something funny happened. I got angry and the next time the referee shouted his Japanese words, I hit the Black Belt first.

This time the arm was raised in my direction and I had the point. I was amazed. We fought for two minutes and the score remained the same, dead level. An extension of a minute was given to fight on. We drew again and a further thirty seconds were allowed. I would like to say I triumphed, but I didn't. The Black Belt beat me, but only by half a point.

I felt strange after it was finished. People congratulated me on my effort and I was disappointed that I wouldn't fight again that day.

However, other tournaments beckoned, and after a couple of belt tests I obtained a yellow belt. I was then entered into a local North Wales tournament. It was not on the scale of the previous one but there were a lot of people there.

Our club made up two teams, and I was first up for the "B" team. Again I was matched against a higher grade. He stormed out and I hit him in the nose. Point to me. Then he punched me, a bit hard and he got a point. So I punched him a bit harder and his nose started to bleed. He complained to the ref, who was also his instructor and I got warned. The fight restarted and I threw a kick, which gave me enough points to give me the fight. I was delighted as it was the first time I had won anything. Sadly, none of the other lads won so our team went out.

I was left to fight in the individuals, which were done in lower and higher grade sections, which was a bit fairer. I won two fights and got through to the semi-finals. I couldn't believe it.

However, my joy was short lived as I was drawn against a new member of our club who had just come out of military service with the Marines. I was totally intimidated. Sean did his best to motivate me.

"Come on Si, you are much better than him." He was probably right, but I didn't believe him, and went into the fight knowing I was going to lose, so of course, I lost.

A small consolation was that I fought again for third place and won. I then came first in the kata section (moves against an imaginary opponent) and for the first time ever, I had won something. I felt so proud of the little tin trophy I was given. For once, I had suppressed my fear enough to actually triumph at something, even if it was just a small, local tournament.

I was now really into training and looked up to Jackie's boyfriend, Sean. He seemed to be everything I wanted to be. He was a Black Belt, with a nice girlfriend and the respect of many. He took me all over the place training, and had started taking me running early in the mornings. I saw him as a friend.

However, even that turned sour. I had an argument with my sister. Nothing serious, just brother and sister stuff. Too siblings falling out over something trivial but Sean, for whatever reason, did not see it this way. He decided to teach me a lesson and it was a short but violent lesson.

He approached me to give me what I thought would be a 'telling off' but his mood quickly turned dark and he started raining punches onto me. My nine stone frame was no match for this grown man. A fifteen stone, well trained 2nd Dan Black Belt International Karate fighter. He annihilated me with his fists, beating me down to the floor. He became even angrier when I refused to stay down, more out of fear that he would do more damage to me if I was lying down, than if I was standing up.

Every time I made my way to my feet he would punch me back to the ground. Eventually his fury subsided when I was sick and covered in snot and tears. Not only had he hurt me physically, he had destroyed my image of him and all I thought he stood for. I was shattered by the event.

As my sister begged me not to tell anyone of the situation, he offered me his hand which I reluctantly took for the sake of Jackie. Sean and I had a grudging coexistence from then on but I saw him for what he was…a bully.

I continued to train with him, but my heart really wasn't into it anymore. Especially when a co-worker told me that he was planning to follow up the beating by teaching me another lesson at the training session that week.

I arrived at the session prepared for more of the same, yet another assault. Sean seemed to enjoy toying with me, putting off sparring with me until the last round, having fought everybody else first. It was as if he enjoyed seeing me suffer, waiting my turn.

I don't know how what happened next did, but it I think it took us both by surprise. As we started to spar, I found some fire in my belly and refused to be humiliated, as he had planned. I was not 'taken to the cleaners' and I fought at such a pace that I matched him punch for punch and, more often than not, beat him to the draw.

Every time he would make his move I would be first. I seemed to be able to read his moves and gave every bit as good as I got, if not better. I was completely comfortable with it all, whilst he just looked surprised and when he bowed at the end of the fight, he also offered me his hand again. I saw a glimpse of respect in his eyes. It was not reciprocal. He had soured me to the thing that I thought would be my salvation and I had lost heart and faith in my training. Despite my victory, this would be the last time I trained with him, and indeed the last time I trained for some years.

Time was rolling on and girls started to play a factor in my life. I was now seventeen and the pubs and clubs beckoned. I was torn between training and having a laugh. I had started dating the girl who had warned me about Jimmy's knife and evil intentions some years earlier.

On a warm summer's evening I stood outside a shop waiting for her for our night out. We were going to have a drink at a nice local pub. The five lads who approached me had other ideas.

I didn't know them and didn't want to as I could spot their menace and intentions straight away.

"I hate that jacket you're wearing!" barked the ringleader.

"Well good job you don't have to wear it then," I retorted.

Any answer, no matter what would not have prevented the violence that followed. I was backed up against a wall, squashed in between a post box and phone box. Forward was my only way out so I launched a knee to his groin. Sadly, at the same time in my panic, I pushed him backwards. I actually pushed him out of the way of my strike!

He laughed and punched me about four times. I was stuck against the wall and fell to the ground where he proceeded to kick me. When he got tired of this, he started shouting obscenities at me. When this too became tiring he let me be, leaving me dazed and once again humiliated on the floor. Two of his friends laughed, but, sympathetically helped me up, just as my girlfriend came around the corner.

I felt useless and embarrassed as she cleaned me up and consoled me. I just couldn't get the hang of this "real" fighting thing and no amount of training was going to change that.

To be fair to Sean, when he found out what had happened, he went mad and went looking for the lads who attacked me.

He gave them a real bollocking and they left me alone after that. I don't know though, if he was being protective of me or if he was just jealous that someone else had beaten me up!

Years later, I still see Sean around from time to time. He and my sister divorced after some years of marriage and our paths do not cross that much anymore.

It would seem he has 'retired' his Karate suit and is no longer the trim fighting machine he once was. I know at one time, his ambition was to open a full time Karate academy, with all the equipment that goes with it. Punch bags, striking shields etc. I suppose very similar to the one that I opened, not a million miles away from where he is now.

I also knew that he wanted to make teaching Martial Arts his career of choice...very similar to what I do now. He never did though, he was never able to make it unlike me. Ah well, Karma will visit us all and she must have known...I don't make it a habit of going around beating up youngsters.

CHAPTER FIVE

I have said from time to time that Karate was my salvation. I am of course wrong. Salvation came to me at the age of nineteen. I met salvation one Sunday afternoon whilst out in my car with some friends. We had stopped at a local Burger King when salvation walked past. Her name wasn't in fact salvation. Her name was Julie.

Things had been moving in an entirely different direction for me that summer. I found friends and popularity when I joined a rock band. Training was now a thing of the past and my nights were spent playing gigs, chasing girls and drinking. Much the same as all the other lads.

All that came to an abrupt end on that Sunday afternoon. Julie was a girl I had known for a couple of years, and been friendly with, before she moved away from the area. I hadn't seen her for quite some time and was delighted with the chance meeting outside the Burger King.

I had always liked her before and still liked her a lot now and when we spoke again I considered asking her out on a date. As I was with my friends, I postponed my romantic endeavor for another time. Well, that, plus I didn't have the nerve to ask her to her face.

So, I gave her a lift home and we said our goodbyes. The lads in the car made the usual noises as she walked away making cat whistles but I ignored them. I drove home at top speed to obtain her phone number from the book. I waited until the next night before plucking up the courage to phone her and ask for a date.

"Hi Julie, its Simon," I said as she answered the phone. I planned to blind her with my charm.

"Who?" She responded, not having a clue who I was, so perhaps blind her isn't the right expression.

"Er, Simon Morrell. We met outside Burger King yesterday," I said, my face reddening.

"Oh. Hi....What do you want?"

"Would you like to go for drink sometime?" I wanted a hole to open up and swallow me up as I prepared to hear her excuse, but she surprised the life out of me.

"Er... yeah okay." The poor girl. What was she thinking? I couldn't believe my luck. And so it was, the following Thursday, a day before my nineteenth birthday and a week before her sixteenth, I found myself with her on our first proper date. After that night it took me a while to convince her to be my regular girlfriend, but it was worth the effort as I started spending more and more of my time with her. She became, undoubtedly, my best friend. The first time I ever needed her to stand by me, she did so admirably.

She would repeat this support so many times later on in life, and through such terrible times, that I often wondered where she got her strength from. When my resolve was weakened, and at one particularly bad time, gone completely, Julie would be behind me gently pushing me in the right direction.

So I should not have been surprised at the first time she showed her strength. It was when I was about twenty. I'd had a run in with some local lads. I want to stress at this point that this wasn't bullying. We just didn't like each other and a row was inevitable.

For reasons that now escape me, abuse was thrown back and forth between us for several weeks with not much coming from it. Then they did something unforgivable.

Julie was out shopping one day, with her baby nephew in his pram. She had nothing to do with my argument with the lads in question, but this didn't stop some of these brave chaps shouting filth at her. The abuse levelled at her was disgusting.

Meeting with her later that day, Julie told me about what had happened. I was so angry. They had an argument with me, no one else, certainly not Julie, and I wanted to put this right.

As coincidence would have it, a couple of nights later I found myself drinking in the same pub as these guys, when I was with my friend Rob. There were about five of them to our two. Good odds for them, so they mustered up a campaign of smart remarks and filthy looks.

"Who are they?" Rob asked, indicating over my shoulder to them.

I explained the situation, and that, quite frankly, I was sick and tired of the bunch.In my mind they had become nothing but cowards.

"Let's go and get Colin, he'll give us a hand," he said with a grin on his face.

We drove to a local snooker hall where Rob's brother, Colin, was having a few games. Rob explained the situation to him and the three of us returned to the pub. I know a lot of people will say we were foolish and should have just gone somewhere else and they are probably right. But how many times, especially in a small town, can you go somewhere else, how many times can you avoid people and situations?

Closing time came around and the inevitable happened as a brawl took place. We drove past the group in Rob's car and as we did, they hurled abuse at us. Rob slammed on the breaks and Colin was out and at them before we could even react. The violence that followed was brutal. He was like a one man fighting machine. On his own he put three of the opposition in hospital.

I think he was so fast he caught them by surprise but once they gathered their wits about them they fought back and the melee was on.

On rushed toward me screaming obscenities with fists swinging. As I began swinging myself, hitting him repeatedly in the face, his friend jumped on my back and hit me from behind, splitting my eyebrow open. His bravery resulted in stitches for me, but for his reward Colin took hold of him. He smashed the lad's face into his rather large knee and the guy was left unconscious on the pavement.

Somebody called the police, and we could hear the sirens approaching. We ran to Rob's car and tried to get away, but were caught by the police some way down the road.

Looking back to where the fight took place we saw bodies everywhere and a couple of girls screaming hysterically. The police took us to the station, and those who needed it were taken to hospital. I was sent there with a stern warning by the

Sergeant, "Be back here at six o'clock tomorrow or you will be arrested"

I had no intention of being arrested, and so the next nigh stupidly I volunteered myself to the local station, without the benefit of a solicitor. There I was asked for my version of events, which obviously differed from our opponent's. I was fingerprinted and photographed and informed that I should expect charges to follow.

"What charges?" I asked, any bravado starting to leave me as it sunk into me that this was not a game or a laugh. This was very, very real with the possibility that one or more of us could be facing jail.

"Well, we are not sure about you, but your mate could be looking at two counts of attempted murder," the Sergeant casually informed me.

The room started to spin. I felt sick at this sudden, dreadful twist.

"What! Attempted murder, it was just a fight!" I justified.

"Try telling that to the two guys still in hospital," I was coolly chastised in return.

Then the reality really sank in. This was going to be a bad time for me. I told Julie what had happened and she laughed and thought I was joking. She still does that now. Always thinks I am joking. I don't know why. However, once she realised I was telling the truth, she rallied around and showed her support and what was developing into love. We went out for a drink but I was so shocked at the possible charges that I couldn't speak all night.

"It will be alright love. They deserved it," Julie consoled me.

"Yeah, but what's my dad going to say?" was all I could manage to reply.

"Tell him everything, he'll understand," Julie suggested.

He didn't. The next day I got up early to catch him at breakfast, hoping my honesty would be enough to convince him to be lenient with me. After all, he knew that there was history between me and the guys in question. He knew I wasn't the kind of kid to engage in violence casually.

The conversation did not go well. He could not, or would not see any side I may have, or even listen to any words I tried to say in my defence.

He screamed abuse at me, hurling foul-mouthed insults and could not resist threatening to kick me out of the house, fire me from the job I had with him and added, for a little bit of spice, the amount of time I would be spending in prison.

"You deserve it you fucking idiot!" were his fatherly words.

For the next few weeks he could not resist jibes and 'jokes' at my expense.

"This time next month you will be banged up in Walton Jail," he laughed one day. This went on and on, as I waited for the charges to come. Colin had already been committed for trial at Crown Court. It wasn't a charge of attempted murder, but three counts of GBH. I waited for my charges to follow but none ever did. I was told by my mum that the police had called and would not be pursuing me. I was light with relief.

This is when my dad tried to 'man up' and offer me some wise words.

"I hope you have learnt your lesson," was all he could say, sounding ever so slightly disappointed.

"Yes," was all I could manage back.

Colin was eventually tried at Crown Court on three charges of Grievous Bodily Harm. All he got was community service. How he managed it, I'll never know.

CHAPTER SIX

In the aftermath of the brawl outside the pub I felt I needed some discipline or 'way' so I decided, with Julie's ever present encouragement to start training again. I would not go back to the Karate club run by my (now ex) brother-in-law and so twice a week made a thirty mile round trip to a new club I had found.

I had also been enlisted by a friend into the local boxing club. The sparring was heavy and it was a long, adrenaline filled drive to the gym every Monday and Friday. Like everyone, I suppose, I struggled with the natural instinct not to turn around and go home.

However, also like everyone, the feeling of satisfaction, and the ever-growing mental strength I felt after each session was well worth any fears I had. I was still a nervous person, I suppose that's in my nature, possibly to always be with me, but I was starting to find some kind of resolve, determination and confidence. This was enforced when I was complimented on my training from both the Boxing Coaches and the Karate Instructor.

I was also very flattered when a friend of mine asked me to go and work as a Bouncer on the doors with him. He had done it for years and the nightclub he worked at was looking to find a replacement for a guy that was leaving. He had been asked to find one and offered it to me first.

As flattered as I was, I also knew that at this time, the pressure would be too much for me. Sure, I was training harder than I ever had before but I still looked at myself as someone who could be bullied. I wasn't sure if I could handle a "real" conflict. I realised that taking this job could be too much too soon. It could lead to massive setbacks to the progress I was making in establishing some confidence.

I was really enjoying the two different types of training but on a personal level, I was fed up living in the same town where I had spent most of my life. It was a small town where everyone knew your business and past.

The whole incident involving the fight and the police, coupled with some other unpleasant experiences, left me wanting to try pastures new. Not the other side of the world, but a new town, a new outlook and new people.

At this time, Julie and I, despite our ever growing love for each other were going through a bit of a rough spell, as all young couples do.

However, things were getting better. We went for a drink one night and I told her we needed to talk. As I was about to start, some friends of ours came in and joined us at our table, interrupting what I had to say to Julie. It could wait until later.

I thought nothing of them joining us and we seemed to be having a laugh. That was until I looked at Julie who was fighting back tears. As soon as I got chance, I asked her quietly what was upsetting her.

"Are you going to finish with me?" she asked.

I laughed, I was so surprised.

"It's not funny," she told me off, getting more upset.

"It is funny," I said, laughing again. "I was going to ask you if you would move in with me!"

More tears of a different type followed and two months later we moved into a lovely little house in the same town where I was now doing Karate. It was close enough for work but far enough for a change of scenery. We were enjoying our life together and decided to take a holiday to Florida. I was really looking forward to going and had been feeling really good. However, I was about to find out how bad I was at handling the slightest little crisis.

It was extremely hot at this time of year and one day whilst waiting in the line for a ride at Disney World, Julie fainted with the heat. It was nothing more than a heat faint. She just simply came over all dizzy and passed out.

Luckily a nurse was standing next to us and came to our aid. Can you believe this? There was a disabled person in a wheelchair nearby. The nurse approached the young lad, and, I swear this is true, asked if we could borrow his wheelchair. He didn't hesitate. His friend helped him out of the chair and onto a nearby bench and the nurse and a ride attendant put Julie in the chair, and we took off like a contestant on a game show.

We rushed though shops and maintenance areas to the first aid bay. The room was full of people who had fainted, just like Julie. She was given a bed, some kind of re-hydration drink and told to rest. After an hour or so she felt a lot better so we returned to our car, and went for something to eat. There seemed to be nothing to worry about.

However, a few days later we were out shopping and went into a bookshop. Julie told me she felt faint again so I rushed her out of there and to the car, panicking. I had to get her back to the hotel, back to what I thought would be safety. To say that I over reacted would be, at the very least, an understatement.

By the time we reached our hotel room Julie was feeling a lot better. I, on the other hand, was in an acute state of anxiety. My mind was working overtime with all sorts of fear fantasies. They came thick and fast with all sorts of illogical questions:

"What if Julie faints again and there is no one to help us?"

"What if she faints and I can't find the hospital?"

"What if she faints and I can't bring her round?"

The "what ifs?" came fast and furious as my head began to spin.

I didn't know how to deal with somebody fainting and I just wanted to go to sleep to escape it all. Julie on the other hand, was coping fine and asked quite logically:

"Shall we go for a swim?"

"God no!" I thought to myself. "What if she faints whilst she's swimming".

I didn't tell Julie what I was thinking. I just said, "No, it's too hot for you. Just stay in the room and keep nice and cool."

She was very good and didn't argue although her idea was probably much better than mine. A cool swim and a relaxing sit by the pool was just what we needed.

However, I felt sick with worry about her and my inability to cope. I fell asleep for a couple of hours and when I awoke it was dark. My worrying had overworked my adrenaline system but it had calmed down so we took a stroll to the bar and I pondered over why I had overreacted so much.

When we returned to our room, I discovered a simple problem that had my panic stations on full alert again. I discovered we had a puncture on our hire car.

"What are we going to do?!" I asked myself, adrenalin at full throttle. I couldn't seem to get a grip. It was after all, only a simple puncture. I scoured the rental agreement for any reference to our problem. Fortunately, according to the agreement, the State of Florida had abolished the death sentence for punctures the year before. But almost as bad, it told me I was responsible for any repairs.

"Don't worry, we'll just get it fixed tomorrow," Julie sensibly advised. The next day I awoke early, having not slept well at all.

"Are we going to get the car fixed this morning?" asked Julie.

"No! I'll go, you stay here in the cool." I snapped at her.

The reality of it was my anxiety was slowly, but surely, growing out of control. I was terrified that Julie would "have a turn" at the garage and we wouldn't be able to get her out of the heat or to get help. Strangely enough, the mechanic was able to fix the puncture. No big deal or panics, just five dollars. After that I spent the last couple of days monitoring Julie and worrying, just waiting for the next crisis to happen.

It did. On the last day, absolute disaster struck. We had about six or seven hours to kill before our plane home so we decided to see a film. Whilst waiting to go to the cinema we were wondering around a shopping centre, buying last minute gifts. All of a sudden, a wave of sickness and heat washed over me. I felt faint and dizzy.

"Christ!" I thought, "Now I'm going to faint!"

"Ju, I'm going for some air, I'll meet you back at the car," I told her. I felt like I was in a dream. Nothing seemed real, it seemed like I was watching a film of myself.

Sitting in the car I was so overcome with panic that my heart felt like it was going to leap out of my chest. I thought I was having a heart attack. The heat was unbearable so I turned the air conditioning on but as soon as it clicked in I shivered uncontrollably, freezing. I needed to throw up as yet another wave of panic ran through me.

Julie returned to the car and turned to me looking worried.

"Are you alright, love?" she asked.

It suddenly occurred to me that that if anything happened to me, Julie would be left on her own. What would she do? Could she cope? This thought produced another wave of panic which in turn was replaced with a more terrifying one. What if she suddenly became ill or fainted? We would both be stranded.

"I'm sorry, I've got to be sick." I told her as I fled from the car to an area behind the shops. There I leaned against the wall, weak and hot. I tried to vomit but hadn't eaten anything all day and so nothing came up. My stomach hurt from the retching and my legs went to jelly.

I thought of the long flight ahead and became convinced I would never make it home. I needed to sit down and staggered to the car. We had nowhere to go for several hours, so we just sat there. I was frozen with fear, heart now beating so fast I could hear it in my ears and feel it inside my head. I just wanted to sleep.

I decided to try and drive somewhere, but I had no idea where. I would take us about two miles up the road looking for sanctuary but I wasn't sure what this meant let alone where to find it. I started to feel worse and did a U-turn and drive back to the shopping centre. I felt like we literally had nowhere to turn.

I started to worry that I would pass out and crash the car and this brought more anxiety. I know people reading this will be saying that I should have done the obvious and just gone to a hospital but I just couldn't think straight. My head felt like it was bursting with the sound of my heart racin

Julie suggested we try and find a motel to rest for a couple of hours. This in itself produced more anxiety as every motel seemed to be booked up. I sat in the car waiting whilst Julie would check the motels for a room. The heat was now unbearable and nausea swept through me. My whole body shook with fear as adrenaline surged through me.

"What the hell is wrong with me?!" I kept repeating in my head. Every time Julie came back to say we couldn't get a room, more adrenaline was released as I became convinced that I was going to die and leave Julie stranded alone.

After some fifteen motels had been checked we found a room. I didn't want to leave the cases in the car but the adrenaline had left me too weak to carry them, so Julie hauled them up the stairs to our room whilst I sat on the bed.

At least the room was cool and I had somewhere to lie down. I felt exhausted and collapsed on the bed. I was asleep within seconds. Later on in life, sleeping was to become an escape for me as this episode would not end here. Rather it would develop into full-blown agoraphobia and ruin years of my life.

However, for now it was enough that I could sleep away the anxiety. Some hours later I awoke and felt a little bit better. It was time for us to go to the airport and this time I could carry the cases. We drove along the highway and came to some traffic lights. Without warning panic took over again. My thoughts seemed to rush through me and I couldn't get them in any kind of order. I struggled to breathe properly. My questions came rushing at me again:

"What if this happens on the plane?"

"Why won't these lights change? I've got to keep moving!"

"Am I going to die or lose control?"

Ridiculously, I considered going into the hotel we were sitting outside and begging the manager to give us a room until I could calm down. This thought only added to my misery as I knew I would sound like a lunatic. Knowing this made me question if I was a lunatic. Was I losing my mind?

It certainly felt like I was. Somehow I kept control and we made it to the hire car depot. Giving up the car was difficult because now we had to sit on a bench on a large open veranda waiting for the bus to take us to the airport, which meant we were in full view of everyone with nowhere to run too.

In other words, we were no longer in control of where we went and how we got there, should I need to "escape" again.

Along with about ten other people we were shepherded onto a minibus and I opted for the back seat by the window. This way I could open the window should I need to. But then I noticed that the bus was filling up and people were moving along the backbench seat next to me to allow others to sit down.

I felt trapped and panicked again. The passengers were laughing with each other and one couple was sharing the story of their honeymoon and their return to Canada.

"Shut up! Can't you see I'm dying?" I wanted to shout. Of course they couldn't. Because I wasn't. What was happening to me was all internal and brought about by my thoughts and reactions. To anybody else I looked fine, maybe just a bit quiet but I felt hysterical. We arrived at the airport and Julie had to carry the luggage to check in. I felt in a state of collapse and the length of the queue did nothing to calm me.

I sat down whilst Julie tried to get us some help. The room was spinning and the voice of the intercom seemed like it was screaming at me. I felt that every person in the place was watching me, seeing me go mad right in front of their very eyes. Julie explained to a British Airways agent that she thought I was seriously ill but the lady was more concerned with hustling passengers to the check-in counter.

"Please! Can you get him some help?" Julie pleaded.

"Just tell him to sit down," the BA representative ordered. "I've got work to do." Splendid service, she must of excelled at her customer care training seminar.

Luckily, a rep from another company could see our distress and came to our aid. She rushed us to the first aid room and called the Paramedics. First to arrive was a Sheriff who had heard of our situation on the internal radios. He looked concerned as he took my pulse.

"You may have picked up a bit of Florida flu," he offered.

"Florida flu! Florida flu! Don't you recognize a heart attack, or a stroke or a brain tumor?!"I wanted to scream at him.

Of course, he was right, but my state of mind wasn't. I was terrified. The Paramedics arrived and started hooking up machinery to me. After a series of tests they concluded that I was fit to fly but should consult with my doctor when I arrived home. They left us in the room with the rep who had bought us something to eat. We still had a couple of hours to wait until we could board our plane so I slept whilst Julie and the rep chatted quietly.

When it was time for us to go to the plane, the rep helped Julie carry our baggage and offered me a wheelchair to the gate. She walked us as far as passport control and radioed ahead to the gate that we were coming to the plane and we should be given priority boarding due to my condition.

It was to my great sorrow that I didn't get this lady's name and company so that I could have written and thanked her properly for her help and concern. She was an angel and I don't know what we would have done without her.

It is a shame that I couldn't say the same for the British Airways staff. When we arrived at the gate we were greeted with the sight of over three hundred people waiting to board the 747 back to the U.K. I sat slumped on the floor whilst Julie informed the staff that we were the couple who were supposed to pre-board.

She was told wait in the queue like everybody else. At this point I was having trouble standing, my legs were that weak from the constant onslaught of adrenalin.

We made our way to the back of the line but luckily an elderly couple near the front of the queue and, apparently aware of our situation, called us over and beckoned us in front of them. I smiled weakly as Julie thanked them for their kindness. This same couple was to show more concern when we arrived back in Manchester.

Whilst I went to the toilet to try and calm down, these two "angels" helped Julie to take our cases off the carousel and onto the trolley.

Another thank you I owe.

After a long and horrible flight, I was delighted to see my sister waiting for us at the arrival lounge. Julie explained what had happened as we drove home to North Wales. I slept on the back-seat as they talked, concerned about me.

I was given a couple of days off work to recuperate. The relief of arriving home safe was soon to be replaced with a growing anxiety of the same thing happening again.

Trips to the doctor's proved unsuccessful as test after test revealed that there was nothing wrong with me. Eventually it was suggested that the problem might be my nerves.

"No," I told myself. "I am not having a breakdown, they are wrong."

They weren't. My complete refusal to accept my illness made things worse as stress chemical after stress chemical flowed through my now shattered body. I lost weight and any self-confidence I had was shattered. I now thought that life had eventually done its worse and had given me the final kick. I became depressed and dreaded going out of the house.

Panic attacks and terrible thoughts took over my life. I would feel trapped when I had a conversation with anybody other than Julie.

Early one Saturday morning I was in the kitchen having my breakfast when there was a knock at the door. It was my Mum and Dad come to visit. I felt sick with anxiety. I was now trapped in the house that had become my safe haven because if I felt a funny turn coming on when my parents where there and I needed to get away, then they would think it rude of me. They had made the effort to come and see me and yet I couldn't really concentrate on what they were saying.

Julie and I had not really told anybody how bad I was. I think this was probably shame on my part and I think we didn't think people would understand. I felt I had hit rock bottom. I was now so bad that, on some mornings, I couldn't even get myself dressed. Julie would wake me up and I would sit like a zombie at the end of the bed whilst she pulled my clothes on. She would then drive me to work and I would sleep again through the whole thirty-minute journey.

When we got around the corner from the factory, she would wake me up again. People who knew I was ill, whilst sympathetic, would sometimes run out of patience with me and quite often I was told to "pull my socks up."

This would add to my growing misery as I began to feel like a complete failure. The bullied person from my childhood was back, only this time it was he himself and life itself that were bullying him. My fear of the outside world grew and I could only go anywhere if Julie was with me. She drove me everywhere.

If we went out for a drink I would have to stand by the doors in case I needed to get out of the room if I was to have a turn. The doctor put my on tranquilizers and I seemed to wander around in a daze. I took the pills reluctantly for a couple of months but at this time Julie had been to a health shop to see if she could get me a tonic to perk me up.

Whilst there, she told the lady behind the counter of my illness. The lady went into the back of the store and came back with a battered old book called "Self Help For Your Nerves".

"Please," she said. "Take it to your boyfriend and ask him to read it. It will help."

Julie came in from work that night to find me lying on the settee. This had become my life. On the days when I couldn't find the strength to go to work, I would wake up in the morning, go downstairs and fall asleep on the settee. This was both from nervous exhaustion and as a form of escapism and yet I would still not accept I had bad nerves so when Julie gave me the book I just looked at her, took it and put it to one side.

"No," I mused, "I'm proper ill. There is nothing wrong with my nerves."

Things got worse. One day I decided to take one of my dogs, Bruno, a large German Shepard for a walk. He really was a gentle giant and loved a run on the college fields behind our house. We had a nice walk and set to cut across the fields on our way home. As we reached them I became aware of how open and big they were. I remembered a story of a local man who had died on the nearby golf course because the ambulance couldn't get to him in time as he was so far out.

"Shit, that's going to happen to me!" I told myself.

Immediately my fight or flight system went into overdrive. The thing about the fight or flight system is that it is a natural asset for the body. When the body senses danger, of any kind, it will release adrenaline into the blood stream. This adrenaline is like a fuel, given to us to enable us to be stronger (for fight) or faster (for flight). Used correctly it is a magnificent piece of machinery.

However, to use it correctly, like anything else, you have to know how to, which I didn't. To me it was just an enormous dose of fear, which turned my legs to jelly. Once again I didn't think I was going to make it home on such weak legs. My head did its usual spinning tricks and I was short of breath. There was no one around to help me. I was going to die, out here with nobody but my dog to see.

I didn't die. I made it home. I always made it home. It just didn't feel like I was going to at the time. Shattered I went back to the settee and slept, too bewildered to stay awake. Why was this happening to me?

One fear would produce another, until I was scared of almost everything. My nervous system had now taken such a battering that the slightest thing could send it into overdrive again.

I became very anxious if I had to have a haircut. My thinking was that if I had an attack halfway through the cut and had to run out of the barbers' then I would not only look an idiot in front of all the customers, but I would be running around with only half a haircut! People were bound to think I was a lunatic.

It was with this fear in my mind that I set off, with Julie driving, to the local barbers. Julie waited outside and as I approached the shop I reached for the tablets the doctor had prescribed for me. Something stopped me taking them out of my pocket… I had no hands.

No, seriously, I remember thinking to myself:

"How bad have I become that I have to take a tablet to have a haircut? Christ, I must be bad!"

I reached for the tablets and threw them down the nearest drain. The fire in my belly that sometime showed itself, as in the case when I would not let my Karate Instructor/ex-brother in law intimidate me reappeared. I would not spend the rest of my life under the domain of a tablet. Not a chance…

Proper help had to be sought out. A psychiatrist if that's what it took. I now accepted that my illness was "bad nerves" and so I took a leap of faith and added a dash of courage. I started reading the book that Julie had got for me. Everything started to fall into place. The symptoms in the book were the symptoms I was having;

 Chest pains, pangs of panic, dizziness, shortness of breath, fear of losing control, fear of going mad. Fear of everything. This book was describing me! It would be difficult, but my recovery would start that day, start with reading that book. I knew it would be a long and tough process, but it had to be done.

I never took another tablet again. My eventual recovery would come from the knowledge that this, and other books, would offer me.

Years later, I realise that life wasn't given to us to waste time worrying it away. We have to make the most of our time, it is precious. Really, you can't laugh too much! Why was I so afraid of half a haircut? Why is that so bad? I was recently having my weekly cut at my friend Dawn's barbershop. To say Dawn likes a laugh is putting it mildly. There is never a dull moment.

Half way through the cut, she had shaved most of my hair but left me with a big tuft sticking up. I looked like the lunatic from the Robert De Niro film "Taxi Driver".

Dawn bet me that I wouldn't walk into a crowded Saturday afternoon supermarket and buy a can of Coke. The rest of the customers looked on amused, baiting me. Never one to refuse challenge, away I went. The staff at the supermarket didn't know what to make of me as I stood with my serious face on paying for my Coke. Children stared and dogs barked as I walked back into the shop to the cheers and smiles of the customers.

Mission accomplished and a free haircut! Also, a room full of smiling strangers. And then it occurred to me. This is what I was scared of all those years ago! Half a haircut!

You can never laugh too much!

CHAPTER SEVEN

Making the initial effort to recover was indeed the catalyst for that recovery. We decided to move house and were lucky enough to find a beautiful new bungalow in a small market town. We lived there for many years before moving on and we loved the house. My two eldest children had grown up there and the best years of my life have been spent there too.

However, even after the move my good health was still a long way away. I made a positive decision to do something about it and went to see my doctor. I think I surprised him by requesting help from a professional.

"A golfer could never help you Simon," he advised.

"No" I retorted, "Professional medical help I mean."

Of course that wasn't really what was said. No, he just referred me to a behavior therapist. My appointment would be a couple of months coming through.

However, somebody was about to enter my life and inspire me to recover in a way I could not have imagined, and in circumstances that to this day both amuse me and inspire me.

I still harbored a burning desire to achieve my Black Belt, and despite everything, refused to believe that my goal was unreachable. I still had a small spark of faith in myself.

However, my state of mind was such that at this time it seemed like a million miles away. I had to take one step at a time. I had to get better and free of my seemingly out of control anxiety first. I still though kept up with the Martial Arts via various magazines on the subject. One such monthly publication had an interview with a Karate-ka turned doorman/bouncer who had written a book about his exploits on the door and how he took on the job to overcome his fears.

I read the interview with interest and decided to order the book from my local store. Coincidentally enough, it came the day I was to see the behavior therapist for the first time. I made plans to collect it after my appointment and made my way to the local hospital.

I entered the reception and approached the lady behind the frosted glass, which housed the front desk.

"Hello, I am here to see Doctor Jones, "I advised her.

"Certainly," she replied "Which ward?"

I gave the name of the ward and her attitude changed completely. She slid the window almost shut and hurriedly dismissed me with directions.

"What a strange attitude she has," I remember thinking, slightly put out by her. And then the penny dropped. She thought I was mad, because of the ward I was going to and the person I was going to see. She not only thought I was mad but also apparently dangerous by the way she shut the window.

I wasn't either mad or dangerous. I was just ill. If staff have this attitude toward people with "problems" then what hope is there. Luckily the behavior specialist didn't think the same. She listened sympathetically to my background, took notes and seemed genuinely caring.

I don't mean to criticize, she was a lovely concerned woman, but it was clear that she was all textbook and no 'real life' experience.

After a while she told me that I was "being silly". She convinced me that anxiety was an emotion not an illness and she was quite right. She concluded I would "be alright" and of course she was right, but it didn't help at the time.

Still, the fact that I had made a positive step started to produce a positive attitude and another appointment was made to see her.

After my appointment had finished, I went to collect the book I had been waiting for, Watch My Back, and looked forward to reading the life story of one of Britain's top bouncers.

Looking at the front cover, I enviously thought about what it would be like to be as tough as this man was and to have no fears.

I couldn't have been more wrong. His story started when he was young and suffering from bullies. He went on to suffer from depression and anxiety but manage to turn his life around and achieve his Black Belt. Even though he did, he still feared violent confrontations, and in his effort to overcome his fears, started to work on the door of some of Europe's roughest bars. Talk about tough!

Yet as he faced his fear face on, he still felt scared but would not give in to his fear. He examined, embraced and then accepted his fears.

I read the book twice in about a week. There was so much to take from it. People I spoke to about it couldn't relate my fear of the outside world to the story of Geoff Thompson's fear of violence but to me, fear is just fear. It makes no difference what you are scared of, you are still scared. The bodily reactions to fear are the same no matter what.

Watch My Back explained this like nothing else I had read or heard before, He spoke of, adrenaline rushes, jelly legs, dizziness etc. Knowing that other people who were not 'ill' felt the same bodily reactions brought home to me that, yes, my fear was out of control, but also that it could be brought back into task with a bit of positive thinking and a lot of courage.

The knowledge that there were people out there, who not only survived fear, but actually conquered and controlled fear left me inspired. As Geoff faced 10,000 maniacs head on, I decided I could face a trip to the barber's (much more dangerous, I thought).

I felt light with relief, the kind of relief I had been looking for, for years. I used my release from fear to seek out a karate gym. Dipping my toe in the water first, I went to watch a session.

"Yeah," I thought, "I could do that again. I'll be scared, sure, but so what? What is the worst thing that can happen to me? I may feel unwell and have to leave but big deal."

However, it wasn't that easy. I joined in the next session but my adrenaline was sky high. As soon as the class started I felt trapped. If I ran out I would cause a fuss, in front of all these strangers. Panic started to set in. Then I forced myself to think of the stories in Watch My Back.

Geoff Thompson had overcome his fears and so surely based solely on the fact that I was much more handsome than he was, I would overcome mine.

Then something peculiar happened. As I distracted my mind from fear, I realised that instead of focusing on my panic, I concentrated on the training and forgot all about being scared or trapped. I started to enjoy myself.

All of a sudden it was time to finish. Far to quickly we were changing back into our normal clothes. I rushed home, delighted to be back training. Julie was waiting with a nice cold beer for me.

"How did you get on love?" she asked, obviously pleased for me.

"Great, I'll definitely go back next week," I said with a grin on my face.

And I did. The next thing I knew I was training three or four times a week, getting fitter and feeling healthy. Instead of walking into the changing rooms at the gym with my head down, afraid to look anybody in the eye and too shy to say hello, I was making friends, laughing and going for a pint with some of the lads after the session.

My body was grateful for the physical exercise and my mind was absolutely ecstatic at the break from worrying. Every session felt like a cleansing with the endorphin release at finishing another class a welcome high.

However, one day the novelty of 'being well' wore off. We were very busy in work and I had been under pressure. This triggered off an anxious spell and I went on full alert listening to my body's stress symptoms, convinced I was 'ill' again.

Without realising it I had started to brood on the possibility that my illness was back. I developed a heavy cold, started getting tired again and was generally feeling lousy.

"This isn't fair!" I would repeat to myself over and over, "I thought I was better."

I searched my soul for what was making me feel this way. I couldn't believe I was starting to go backwards, back to the bad old days of lying on the settee, hopeless. For a couple of days I tried to fight off the feelings and banish the anxiety but it was stronger than I was.

And then the penny dropped. I don't know what made me realise it but when I did I laughed out loud. I wasn't feeling 'ill' I was just having everyday stress.

It was a natural if unpleasant feeling and everybody gets it. Just because I was anxious did not mean I was ill. I had thought that by being "better" I would never again feel the churning stomach, worry and occasional depressions. But this isn't the case. The only people who don't have these feelings are dead people and I certainly wasn't one of those (although this was subject to confirmation when people saw me work!)

What I came to realise was that because of pressure at work I was feeling at a low and this would pass. I was not feeling anxious or panicky for no reason as before, I was just having a stressful period, which is part and parcel of modern living. We all suffer it for varying reasons at various times be it an extra workload, a forthcoming test or working to a tight deadline.

It was like having a weight lifted off my mind when I realised I had just joined the ranks of the "normal" people, feeling real stress at a real situation. If I hadn't have felt so bad I would have felt great!

So I accepted the situation for what it was and got on with things. Within a couple of days things had calmed down and I felt relaxed again. The anxiety had gone without me trying to fight to banish it, which would have made the situation worse.

With this in mind, I was able to concentrate on what I loved doing, which was training. The next thing I knew, I was back in competitions and took the initiative to travel away from home, to compete, taking some of the lads from the club with me.

At one of these competitions, some of our lads from the club where a bit intimidated by a team from a big city club but I remember thinking to myself:

"No chance!' I'm not letting anyone frighten me. I'm as good as these." My inner spark had been well and truly lit!

I got matched against one of the big city guys and, despite his team screaming abuse at me, I ignored them and beat their fighter, giving him a few "digs" on the way.

I then realised, it was all about attitude. Of course, ability does come into it, but someone with less ability could quite easily beat someone better, if he forces his will onto him. If you let yourself get intimidated by a fighter, then he's won that fight already. This is true in any stage or walk of life.

I don't mean don't feel fear, you have to have fear. But being fearful and allowing yourself to be intimidated are two different things altogether. If I had allowed my opponent to intimidate me, I would have been too scared to fight to the best of my ability.

Instead, by not really caring for his loud mouth mates, or his bad attitude, I took away some of his power and won the fight. I was starting to get the hang of this!

As well as the tournaments, there were the belt tests to take. I had taken a few and was now a brown belt. It wouldn't be long before I would take the test for Black Belt. My life's goal was getting nearer by the day.

The trouble was, now that I was enjoying a bit of pressure, and coping with it well, I was too settled in the system that I was training in. I felt comfortable there but the fighting was very "touch" contact and never really mentally stretched me.

I was grateful for the confidence this gym and system had given me, but somehow I felt I needed more. I felt no challenge and realised I had stopped growing.

Some weeks after achieving my brown belt, I went to watch Julie at her grading (she had recently started training herself).

There were about forty people attempting various belts. After about a half-hour test, Julie achieved her blue belt. I gave her a congratulatory hug but sensed something was wrong.

"What did you think then? Are you pleased with yourself?" I asked her on the way home.

"Not really," she replied in her usual totally honest fashion.

"What do you mean?" I asked her.

"I didn't deserve it. I felt I could have done anything up there and still passed. It just didn't feel right."

I admired her for her honesty and expected nothing less from her but judging by some of the people at the grading, she was right.

"Well, I've felt like that for some time myself," I told her. "There's no challenge at that club. I have to be straight Ju, I would rather try for my Black Belt at a tougher club. I've come too far for this. I need to know myself that I've got to earn it."

Instead of the usual celebratory drink that follows a success, we just went home to have a good honest look at ourselves. I knew of a guy that taught a traditional style mixed with freestyle fighting and he had always told me that his club was a good, tough one and that I was always welcome there.

So one Monday night I went to see him. "Sure Simon, you are more than welcome," he told me when we met. "What grade are you?"

"Brown belt," I answered him.

"Yeah well, you can train here but just don't wear your belt. I'll tell you when you can wear it."

I thought this a bit strange but, out of respect, went along with his wishes. Looking forward to the first session with him I was disappointed upon arriving at the dojo to find him huddled around the canteen gas fire, smoking a cigarette.

"Mandy is taking the session tonight. I've got a cold," he told me.

"Wow! He is tough," I thought to myself sarcastically.

My disappointment grew as the session turned out to be a lukewarm one. The club I had just left was tougher than this one.

"It will get better when Mike takes the class," I told myself.

Six weeks later, Mike was still sitting in the canteen, smoking.

"Does Mike ever take the class?" I asked one day. I didn't mean to sound cocky, I was just interested. At the end of the day, I was still paying good money to train.

His wife gave me the sort of look that people reserve for bad smells.

"'I'm not being funny Simon, but if Mike sparred with you, he would kick you out of the ring. He's trained in Manchester you know."

"How strange," I thought. I never asked would he spar me, just does he teach. Further, the dojo didn't have a ring so what exactly was I going to get kicked out off? And what did Manchester have to do with anything. A very bizarre thing to say!

However, apparently, the battle plans were drawn. My next visit to the club was met with a rare sight. Mike without a cigarette in his mouth.

"I'm taking the class tonight" he told me as I walked in.

"Good," I thought, finally what I am paying for.

"Tonight it is freestyle (sparring) and street defence," he announced, sending a glance my way.

Brilliant, just what I wanted. He started taking us through the session and well, to be honest, he was crap.

Now bear with me if you think I am being too cocky and judgmental, but you will find I am vindicated at the end of this little story.

He told us to partner up and instructed one of his top students to fight me.

"Don't kill him John," he shouted to his student insulting me from across the room.

"Chance would be a fine thing," I thought, angrily.

Now John is a good guy and extremely good at what he does. Also, he is a nice guy and looked uncomfortable at his 'Sensei's' remarks.

However, a spar is a spar and by this time, I was no mug. Nobody killed me, and I gave better than I got, much better.

So Mike changed the class to street defence. The attacker tried to 'mug' us with a very slow step and punch and we had to side step and, spinning round twice like a ballerina, ending up behind our opponent and hitting him in the back of the head.

Thankfully this little trip into fantasy ended quite quickly and I walked out, disappointed.

I gave Julie the news as soon as I got home.

"Forget it, he's a joke. He is never a Fourth Dan in a million years." My search for a decent club resumed.

Was I right about him or just cocky and arrogant? Well, I'll give you the facts and you decide:

Some years later his governing body, in a dispute over the grades he claimed to hold, found him guilty of misconduct. He was subsequently banned from teaching Karate. This was reported in the press. Since then, he left town and I haven't seen him since.

It is just a shame that his governing body never spotted this earlier, saving thousands of pounds in training fees for students who couldn't see what I thought was obvious.

However, having put so much faith in training, for me personally, the immediate future was looking a bit bleak. I just couldn't seem to find a club that could give me what I was looking for.

I visited most of the clubs in my area and further afield but they were all teaching pretty much the same thing. I am not saying it wasn't any good, not at all. In fact some of it was very strong.

It's just that a lot of the clubs concentrated on one aspect of training, namely kata (a series of moves against an imaginary opponent).

I had enjoyed kata for some time but preferred a more hands-on contact style. A little bit rough and ready, with lots of sparring. I still felt the need to test myself, and so desperately wanted to achieve my Black Belt, but in a style or system that would really push me.

I felt a depression coming on, and started to feel a bit lost. We were due to go on holiday to a lovely log cabin hidden away on the Scottish border. It was a four hour drive and when we arrived, I felt it was just what I needed. I could do some training and try and sort myself out. However, my euphoria was very short lived.

I awoke early the first morning and "bang!" From nowhere I was engulfed by panic, the type of panic I hadn't had in years. It frightened the life out of me. I had no idea why I was getting this feeling again.

"No!"my brain seemed to scream. "We are so far from home and in such a remote area. What if something happens to me?"

I had to get home and quick. I couldn't face Julie. She had been looking forward to this for so long. With my back turned, I muttered to her.

"Ju, I want to go home."

She sat up concerned. "What's the matter?"

"I feel dreadful. Go and pack while I have a nap, please," I pleaded.

"Of course I will," There was no trace of anger or disappointment, just concern "But I think if you are poorly, then this is the best place for you. You should have a good rest".

I said nothing and Julie went off to pack. About an hour later I woke from a snooze and sat quietly thinking to myself. I would stay, but it would be better if we didn't unpack just in case I wanted to go home in a hurry.

This was classic fight or flight (stay or run) syndrome. Julie, as usual, agreed and we went for a walk. I tried to explain how I felt but how could I? I didn't even know myself. Here I was with a beautiful wife, a lovely daughter, my two large dogs, walking in a lovely remote forest, surrounded by all the beauty nature had to offer and I still wasn't happy.

This made me feel worse, because I know some people never go anywhere and this made me feel so ungrateful.

We decided to go for a drive and whilst Julie enjoyed the scenery I tried to analyze how I felt. Deep down, I thought that my dream of being a Black Belt, the thing that had driven me most of my life and the answer to all my demons, was slipping away. I had nowhere decent to train and the fear was back.

I knew I didn't want any old Black Belt that some less unscrupulous gyms could 'guarantee' you. I wanted a good worthy one. I needed to feel proud of it or to not have it at all. I thought back to Watch My Back and tried to think of what Geoff Thompson would have done. I drew a blank. I needed to think what I should do instead.

And then it hit me. I don't know how or what bought it on, divine inspiration? But I knew what had to be done.

I had seen an article in a magazine for the former World Kickboxing Champion Alfie Lewis inviting brown belts to open their own clubs under his banner.

I was a brown belt, I could open my own club and train the way I wanted to. I just hadn't thought of it before. I was ecstatic at this notion.

But there he was, sitting on my shoulder…you know the guy, we all know him:

The bastard that tells you that you aren't good enough. Our inner Mr Negative, the voice that keeps the special person inside us all un-special.

"Probably right, what the hell was I thinking of?" I told myself.

And then the good guy on my shoulder kicked in to argue the point. The guy who dares us to be different, the guy who wants us to be great. The inner voice we should all listen to.

"Tell him to 'do one'!" he commanded me.

"Who?" I asked him/myself.

"That clown who keeps you down. The one that won't let you think you can be good at anything. You are good enough. Come on, you can do this!"

Julie looked at me, concerned that I had a person sitting on each of my shoulders.

"Who are they?" she asked.

No, really, I looked at my beautiful, lifelong best friend and wondered how to bring this up. I was still a doubter. She'll laugh if I tell her what I'm thinking of doing. I had no right to think such I thing. But she didn't laugh. Far from it.

"That's a brilliant idea!" she enthused.

"Well, we'll see," I mumbled.

"No Simon, you are good enough to do this. Where have you seen the advert?"

"I think it was in Fighter's magazine." I replied.

Mr Negative, sitting on my shoulder started to look thoroughly fed up, as Mr Positive realised he had himself a beautiful ally in Julie.

Something happened to me that day in those hills. I have difficulty explaining it, but for the first time in years, maybe for the first time in my life, I felt that I had truly found my way. I felt I had a purpose.

Christ, I could be somebody. Yeah okay, only a brown belt, starting his own Karate club , but I had never been a brown belt starting his own Karate club before.

"Dear me. I was going to be a Karate Instructor!"

I felt I knew enough to get started, and there were courses and training sessions in which I could further my knowledge.

I could add to my sessions, my experience in boxing, in which I had fought many rounds at a local club. I had fought in many tournaments and could add this experience as well.

I had been graded to advance level in two styles of Japanese Karate, and trained extensively in Modern Freestyle Karate, so why shouldn't I try for it?

We went for a drink and talked of nothing else. I knew that Alfie Lewis was a fantastic martial artist and that he also held fair but arduous black belt tests. But would the association except me? I didn't know but by Christ I was going to try and find out!

We cut the holiday short by a couple of days, but this time for positive reasons. On arriving home, we scoured all the old magazines looking for the article. And then we found it and with Mr Negative reading it over my shoulder self-doubt set in again.

Julie wouldn't allow him to get a hold though.

"Here, give it to me I'll phone them and get the info," she told me.

I listened as she spoke to a gentleman named Peter Lewis and explained my situation. He asked to see proof of my training, certificates etc and said that when he got them he would consider my application.

It was a long week waiting for the news and then one day, in the post, came my acceptance letter and Instructor's certificate.

I immediately went to work, rounding up friends to be my first students. I also went into overdrive in training for my Black Belt test, which was going to be in about a year. Peter Lewis had explained the format and what would be expected of me.

I was training six times a week, with running, bagwork, sparring, fitness testing etc. My self-esteem went through the window. People training with me and being taught by me were surprised.

They commented on how good they thought the club was and how well I trained and fought. We attracted some coverage in the local press, which was a good boost for the club.

Some local, disgruntled instructors didn't like the new, modern approach I gave to my club. They, in my opinion, behaved like children with their malicious rumor spreading and trying to close my clubs down. I would not be dragged down by them. They were showing themselves up for what they were and doing themselves no favors.

One particular instructor made some very unkind, untrue, comments about me in the local press and then some weeks later whilst talking on the phone to a mutual friend and a Black Belt Instructor asked what I was like.

"Simon's a smashing lad and very good at what he does," my friend informed.

"Well, I can't really comment on him, I've never met him," replied the guy who had bad-mouthed me.

"Well you should have thought about that before you gave him the bad mouth," submitted my friend.

I tried to ignore their pettiness and trained for the ever looming Black Belt grading. I read everything that Geoff Thompson wrote. His stuff was real down to earth, streetwise self-protection and he was rapidly becoming a role model and inspiration. He was what I was striving to be. Hard when he needed to be but for the most, a generous, inspirational gentleman. He was everything I thought Sean had been all those years ago but turned out not to be. Geoff was, by all accounts, everything I stood for in life.

I threw everything into training for my Black Belt. I had never been fitter, stronger or healthier. And then it all came crashing in...

CHAPTER EIGHT

It was a Saturday night and I had just finished my usual two hour session. My grading was now just a few months away and I was starting to get nervous. I lay in the bath, letting the hot water soothe my aching muscles and thought to myself how near I was to my dream.

Physically I was ready. However, I didn't realise how far I was away mentally. I was imaging walking into the grading room, warming up and then turning to Alfie Lewis ready to start.

And then it hit me. This was real and this was going to happen very, very soon. I felt sick. The questions came at me thick and fast and again I couldn't control the negativity that was starting to get a grip:

"What if I froze on the day?"

"What if I wasn't good enough?"

"What if I got laughed out of the room?"

"What if I had to fight some monster of a guy?"

"Who was I trying to fool?"

I got out of the bath, shaking and panicking. I was going to have to travel to Manchester to grade and what if I became so scared that I became ill and couldn't get home, couldn't escape.

Fear. Fear. Fear.

It had got its ugly claws into me again and this time it wouldn't let go. With shame in my voice, I went to see Julie in the living room. Here it came again, excuses not to do the thing I wanted to do:

"Julie, I'm pulling out of my grading," I muttered.

"What?" Julie couldn't believe it, she was stunned, "Why?"

"I don't feel well. I feel a bit panicky Look, I'm not good enough for this. Let's just leave it okay."

"No, Si, you are good enough. You are more than good enough. I don't know anybody who trains like you. Don't pull out now. This is what you want. You have worked so hard for this." She was imploring me on, a desperate attempt to urge me not to give up on myself.

I couldn't look at her. Mr Negative was sitting pretty on both my shoulders and he had company. Every person who had ever bullied me was with him, along with every panic attack I had ever had. And they all had control of my head.

Mr Positive had had his butt kicked and had left town. For good.

Julie tried again:

"Read some of Geoff Thompson's stuff again. What about the Fear book? That should help."

"No, I've read them all. They can't help" (sacrilege!) "Nothing can help."Oh dear, was I feeling sorry for myself! Julie watched concerned as my eyes filled up with tears.

"Let's just forget it," I muttered.

For a week I half trained, confused, scared and dazed. My heart wasn't in it. What was the point? A deep depression came over me and Julie looked on, worried. I would not take the Black Belt test, which doomed me to a life of failure.

However, I may have given up on myself but Julie refused to do the same. She believed in me, she believed in my dream and she was going to make sure it happened. Giving up on me is not an option for her.

She gave me the surprise of my life and at the same time helped me make a great friend.

One Saturday morning, we were lying in bed talking. Our phone rang and we both thought it was unusual for someone to be phoning this early. Julie didn't get to it in time and so dialed number recall. It was a number neither of us recognized.

An hour or so later, the phone rang again, except this time the caller didn't hang up at the answer phone, but started to leave a message.

I just caught a male voice say, "Hello Julie, hello Simon it's…" but Julie jumped up and ran to the phone picking it up before the caller identified himself.

I was a bit concerned and followed her into the living room where I caught the tail end of a conversation.

"…he's here now. Oh, you sure you don't mind? Thank you very much!"

She looked at me with her lovely concerned eyes.

"Don't go mad will you?" she asked.

"What?... Who is it?... What's going on?..." I asked, confused.

"It's for you. It's Geoff Thompson." She fell silent and handed me the phone. I didn't understand. Tentatively, I took it from her as she left to wait in the kitchen.

"Hello," I said into the mouthpiece.

"Alright mate, it's Geoff Thompson. How are you?"

I had no idea how I was other than I was totally confused by all this. Why somebody would choose to play a cruel joke like this, pretending to be my hero calling me on a Saturday morning? Who was this really? I didn't know how to react.

"Er…fine".

"Listen," the voice said, "You've got a Black Belt test soon haven't you?"

I don't know, did I?

"Er….. yeah" I managed.

"I just want you to know, how brave I think you are. I really believe in you, you going to be alright you know." It started to dawn on me that this was indeed Geoff Thompson, the man whose stories and philosophies had inspired me through the pages of his book.

"How did you know? About the grading I mean"? I asked.

"Julie wrote to me and told me all about your past and the troubles you have had. I can't believe you've come so far.

Crikey you have done well. And as for your wife, she really loves you Si. I can see that from the letter. It's full of love".

I found it difficult to speak and had a huge lump in my throat.

"You are struggling to do it, aren't you?" he continued.

"Yes," I admitted.

"I get scared like that. It is natural. I'll tell you what though. You'll do it. I believe in you and Julie believes in you. You've just got to believe in yourself. We are here for you and we can show you the way but only you can do it. Only you can walk through the door, as much as we would love to do it for you. It doesn't matter if you pass or not. The victory is taking the grading, getting onto them mats. Beating your fear."

I was close to tears. I'd never felt anything like this before, never been so inspired. I could feel the love from this man down the phone and the love from Julie filling the house. Here was my hero, taking the time to help someone he had never even met. We talked for about an hour and I listened as he fed my need for help with his support.

"I'm your friend Simon, I see so much of myself in you. You'll be fine. You just have to find your courage."

And right there and then, I knew he was right. I would take the test, pass or fail. It didn't matter. I had taken tests before, sometimes not knowing they were tests.

When severe agoraphobia had me in its grip I was tested walking out of my house. When panic attacks threatened to engulf me, my willpower to keep going, stay alive, was tested.

At times I thought my sanity was tested. Yes, I would take the test. And when I did, I would write to this fine man and thank him for his courtesy and his hand of friendship and who knows, one day I might meet him.

"I'm here whenever you want, Si. If you need me phone. If I'm out leave a message and I will phone you right back."

I was choked by his gesture. When the conversation came to an end, I was on an all time high. I hugged Julie and thanked God for her. I trained like a demon again.

Also, I couldn't believe I had got a 'once in a lifetime' opportunity to speak to a man of Geoff's caliber. But I was wrong. It wasn't a once in a lifetime call. When this man meant he was your friend, he was your friend. Two days later, before my birthday, he telephoned me again.

"I've lost your address Si and I've got a birthday present for you," he said.

I was shocked. He sent me one of only ten copies in Britain of the USA version of Watch My Back. About a week later he phoned again to give me a top up of inspiration. He was becoming a bit of a pain, I was going to have to change my phone number (you can bet your life I'm only joking there!).

My drive for black belt was becoming unstoppable. I was becoming filled with an energy the likes of which I had never had before. My time was getting nearer…

CHAPTER NINE

The months passed by and I awoke, one sunny Saturday morning knowing this was one of the biggest days of my life. My dad picked us up and I brimmed with confidence, as, safe in the knowledge that Julie and Geoff believed in me, we headed north to Manchester to the grading centre.

I was the only person from my club taking the test so would perform all my basics on my own, with just Alfie Lewis watching.

We arrived at the centre and settled down for a cup of tea whilst the formalities were taken care of. As we sat down I felt the ever so familiar tinge of panic start to take hold.

"No!" I told it. I switched the panic off by letting it know that it had no place with me today. It would not find room to sink its claws into me so it was jolly well wasting its time!

"Fair enough!" it seemed to say and it left on the next bus out of town.

There was a great camaraderie amongst the people waiting to grade. Everyone had hints and tips for each other:

"Show respect, Simon. It is important."

"Drink plenty of water. Don't be afraid to ask for a quick break for a drink."

"If you are unsure of anything, ask! Don't just stumble through to get it over with quickly."

I was very grateful for the advice and support given to me by a guy taking his 3rd Dan, whom I had only just met.

I paced nervously and then my name was called.

"Simon, it's time," Peter Lewis informed me.

I turned to Julie. It was time to banish my demons. It was time to make a stand for myself. I'd waited for this for years. I knew a Black Belt wouldn't turn me into Superman, but it would be one of the toughest situations I had ever had that I wouldn't be running from.

People shouted words of good luck and my Dad patted my back.

"Good luck son," he told me.

As I was about to go, the 3rd Dan shouted me back.

"Simon, a drink," he said passing me a bottle. I nodded my thanks and walked toward the grading room. A couple of people patted my back as I passed and I felt very emotional.

"This is really happening Simon!" I told myself "You are doing this. You are really doing this!" The hairs on the back of my neck were standing up and adrenalin rushed through my bloodstream. I felt great!

I also felt like I was floating, nothing seemed real and what I was seeing was what I saw in my mind's eye several months previously when I had been sitting in my bath as the panic set in. Only this time, I was enjoying it. I warmed up and then Alfie called me to start.

Basics first; blocks, defenses, etc. Then some basic kicks and punches. Then we moved onto more complicated combination techniques. Halfway through, I messed my moves up. I simply went blank for a second. I was given one more chance but panic had set in. The combination was read out but my mind was lost, I couldn't understand what was being read out.

"I'm sorry, I don't understand." I said, trying to be honest, hoping this may go in my favor.

"Neither do I!" laughed Alfie "I just realized. I read it out wrong. Just relax, you are doing fine."

He read the combination out again correctly and this time I understood him. After what seemed like hours, the basics were complete.

"Thank you, you can go," he told me.

My relief was enormous and I grinned as I arrived back to where we had made camp.

"You okay Si?" somebody, I can't remember who, asked.

"Yeah, fine," I said, filled with relief.

"Just the fighting to do now then," said my 3rd Dan friend.

Ahhhhh! I had forgotten all about that!

A long two hours passed as we waited to be called to fight. There were about twenty five of us in the room and Alfie would pick fighters out at random. When it was your turn, you would glove up, step up onto the mats and stay there for several fights against different opponents every time.

My first fight was against a Kick Boxer from Newcastle. He was a lot heavier than I was with some very good techniques.

I got caught with a punch to the jaw and then he followed up with a cracking round kick to the face.

My jaw clicked and my ears rang from the blows. I felt drained but I knew I had to come back with something, so battled on forcing him backwards with kicks to the body.

Then time was called and the lucky bugger got to sit down. We touched gloves with mutual respect and he hugged me.

"Good luck," he said in my ear as my next opponent stepped onto the mats.

I wanted to stand out and so went after him right from the start. I pressurized him and, in his hurry to get out of the way, he stumbled to the floor at the same time as I swept his legs from under him.

I was about to step back and give him space to get up but thought better of it. I rushed forward and hit him with a controlled punch whilst he was on the floor. On impact I screamed "Kiaaaa!!!"

He looked a bit frightened and I could hear some murmurs of approval from the onlookers. He got to his feet a little bit shaky and I went after him again. I was head hunting, confident, strong again and in control of the fight.

Suddenly, time was called and I was told to sit down.

"Thank goodness for that!" I thought, thrilled that it was over, as I undid my gloves.

"No, leave them on!" whispered the guy next to me.

"Oh shit, it must be a sign of disrespect to take the gloves off before being told," I thought.

And then the penny dropped. People who had fought before were being called back up.

"Shit, we have to fight again," I realized. My body gave me a kick off adrenaline that I struggled with.

"Come on, get it together!" I willed myself.

We were watching two lads go at it, when one of them took a particularly nasty knock to the face and ended up falling into the wall, giving his head a nasty crack.

Everybody felt for him. Well everybody except one. A lone voice sniggered and every eye in the room turned on him.

"You shit," I thought to myself. Yes, the gradings are hard and we all get a smack or two. After all, that's what it's about, isn't it? But you don't laugh at another's misfortune. You just don't.

Alfie Lewis looked on quietly as the fight continued, fully aware of what had happened.

On its completion he summoned the 'laugher' up to fight. The lad got pasted. He couldn't box eggs. His fight ended and a fresh opponent was called for.

"No," the lad complained, "I'm going to be sick. I can't go on."

Alfie looked on in contempt.

"If you are going to be sick, then be sick. This is a Black Belt grading, if I was your Instructor I would be furious with you for that. My lads are taught that they only stop fighting for two reasons. Either when they are knocked out or when I tell them to stop. Now if you are going to be sick, be sick and get on with it. You can be sick on the mats."

The guy carried on but his heart wasn't in it and when time was called, he looked very relieved.

I was up again next and realised this was my last fight. This was my last chance to make a good impression. I went for it. I knew I was fit and again headhunted the guy I was fighting.

He backed off from my long reach and just when I thought I had him, he caught me full on with a spinning back kick. The wind sailed out of me and everything in me wanted to go down. Everything but my will power.

I wasn't going down, no way. A strange feeling came over me. I could literally feel all the running and training I had done start to pay off and my second wind came to me at around about the same time as my opponent's left him. I finished very strong and we hugged afterwards. This time when I sat down, the gloves came off and stayed off. Pass or fail I had taken a very hard test, one that years ago I could never have imagined taking.

The last of the fights finished and we were told to put warm clothes on and a drink and to be back in five minutes for our results.

I left the room to find Julie and our little girl waiting and they both gave me a hug. The last guy I fought showed he was a very big man, and for me showed what all the good in Martial Arts is about, when he went out of his way to congratulate me. He then punched me in the back of the head (no he didn't, I just couldn't resist the temptation to write that!) ☺

"Well done, that was excellent," he offered. I returned the compliment and he walked away, back to his camp.

Whilst I was getting my tracksuit top on, two men approached Julie.

"He did well, very well," they told her both nodding genuine approval. I started to feel a bit emotional again.

"Christ, maybe I've passed," I fantasized. "Just maybe I am a Black Belt!"

We lined up to go back in for our results and my heart sank as word came back:

"Someone has failed" the guy in front of me informed me. I knew I had forgotten my combinations and was sure it was me.

We were told to sit down and to only stand up when our name was called. If we had passed, we were to come forward to receive our certificate. If you had failed, well, just sit down again I suppose.

I listened frantically for my name. We were getting nearer and nearer to the end of the list and I still hadn't been called nor had the name of the failure. It was me, I knew it was. I had failed…

"Simon Morrell!" Alfie shouted out.

My nerves were in absolute overdrive as I stood up with familiar jelly legs, dreading what was to come.

"When did I last see you training?" he asked.

"Shit," I thought, "He thinks I haven't trained enough."

"On the summer training camp," I mumbled.

"Pardon?" he said.

Before I could answer, Peter Lewis spoke up:

"Simon was on the summer camp in September," he offered.

"Oh yeah, I knew I knew you from somewhere. Well done, pass with a B. You did very well!" he grinned.

Applause rang in my ears as I strode forward (yes, now

that I was a Black belt I had taken to striding everywhere!) I trembled, as I shook hands with Alfie Lewis and he handed me my certificate. I couldn't take my eyes off it and barely heard any of the other marks being issued to people.

All except for the last mark. Everybody heard it and the room went quite. The guy who had laughed at the fighter banging his head had failed.

He was being brought to task about his fitness, his fighting and his general attitude to the grading. He had chosen to wear a football top to grade in and this didn't go down well. Lack of respect, you see.

I was glad I had worn the correct uniform, correct protective equipment and had a bag full of borrowed spares, just in case.

"It shows that you aren't here mentally," Alfie chastised. "This is a discipline, same as the army. You wouldn't turn up for the army in the wrong clothes would you?"

"No," the lad answered, head down, demoralized.

"You need a vast improvement before you will get your certificate," he was warned.

I didn't care. I had passed and had achieved my lifetime's ambition. I hugged Julie tightly. She had been my very backbone.

My Dad came up with a sweatshirt he had just bought me. It was a black one with the badge of the association on it. The rule was, only black belts were allowed to wear them. I felt so proud.

We were told we could go and a cheer went up. Smiles all round, shaking of hands and fighters hugging fighters.

We were Black Belts.

On the way home, a bottle of champagne was produced by Julie. Again, she was always thinking one step ahead. My relief was indescribable. I felt mentally strong. Surely now, my life was on the right track. I'd had my more than my fair share of adversity, and, so I thought, there would be no more. Life only has so many tests to go around and mine were complete. Yes?

Hell no! Adversity hadn't finished with me just yet. It would seem it hadn't even started. The biggest battle of my life was just around the corner and would come from a most unexpected source. It would be a battle that would change my life forever and force me to question everything I had learnt, everything I had trained for. It would steal all my energy and at times, I thought, would steal my sanity and my life.

It would put a massive strain on my family life and take me lower than I had ever been and yet I would learn so much more about myself.

I would learn that when it mattered, when it really, really mattered, I did have what it takes to "dig deep" and dig deep I did.

CHAPTER TEN

Things started to look very bright for us in the summer of 1996. Julie was pregnant again, we had our adorable little girl, another one on the way and we were running our own successful business renting out bouncy castles for children's parties and fun days.

For me, things had never been better. I had become good friends with Geoff and had been accepted as an Instructor into the association that he runs, along with leading Martial Artist and all round gentleman, Mr Peter Consterdine.

The British Combat Association is possibly the most respected of Martial Art bodies in the world and has instructors and training methods from all spectrums of the combat world. I was honored when they accepted me as an instructor and in my time with them, feel I have grown more than at any other time in my Martial Art's life.

Julie and I worked hard at our business and had very good relationships with our customers and a fine reputation.

However, after seven years of running it, it was time to move on. Now that I was a Black Belt, I felt it was the right time to open my own gym. I envisioned a centre for all types of Martial Arts, with punch bags, weights, fitness equipment and the likes of. The only problem now was the getting the money to start it.

Julie and I talked and both agreed it was a feasible project. I certainly had the work ethic, and Julie backed me 100%. Now I needed to find suitable premises and, of course, the capital to finance the business. It was decided to put our rental business up for sale and our accountant valued it at £17,000.

From just word of mouth, we had a couple of interested parties, one of which surprised us completely.

It came from our neighbor and friend Nick. He had been our neighbor for about eight years. He ran a successful business and seemed a hard working man. More importantly, he appeared to have the money to buy us out, so when he asked if he could buy the business, we were happy to discuss it with him.

The usual negotiations took place, with an offer from him, a counter offer from us before we agreed a sum of £15,000, which would buy him six year's customer base, the company van and all the equipment, which was worth about £9,000.

Included in the £15,000 he was going to give us was a small car he had for sale, which Julie was going to have. We shook on the deal and he arranged to deliver the car the next day. He was due to take control of the company two weeks later when he could arrange to pay the first of three agreed installments.

Julie naturally looked forward to the next day and the delivery of her new wheels, but what happened the next day should have been an omen for us. I arrived home from work and was disappointed to see there was no new car on the driveway. Disappointed but certainly not suspicious, I just put it down to one of those things. I called on Nick who apologised and said he had had a hectic day, which, given his businesses, I could believe.

He promised to bring the car the next day, only to then tell us the next day that his mate had let him down and he had no one to drive it back from his dad's car showroom. I offered to do it but he promised he would take care of it.

Julie and I were working hard winding down our side of the business, getting the database and paperwork together for him, making sure the equipment and vehicles were clean and in working order. On top of this we were looking for premises and equipment for our new gym. It was hard work but exciting. It felt good and something that we were meant to do.

The next day Nick knocked on the door looking a bit shamefaced.

"Sorry Si, I tried to drive the car home and the cam belt went on it. I'm having it fixed before Julie gets it," he offered.

That was fair enough as far as I could see and discussions moved to completion of the deal. A date was agreed for the following Friday for him to take the equipment and we certainly looked forward to the £5,000 in cash he was bringing.

A car sale was how he was raising the money and his buyer had agreed to pay that week. We had seen a suitable location for our gym, arranged for suppliers of equipment and goods and would tie things up on all of that with the money Nick was bringing. The week dragged as we waited for Friday to come along.

Eventually it did and we waited for Nick. However, when he came to us, so did his next set of excuses.

"The man who wants my car can't get the money until tomorrow so I'm just off to dad's to borrow it from him," he explained.

With that he was gone and returned about two hours later.

"My bloody dad is a miserable sod. He says he hasn't got any cash to loan me, but no worries, I'll have it tomorrow. Listen, can I still take over today, I'm really looking forward to this. I promise, I'll have the cash tomorrow afternoon."

I thought about it. He was a good friend, and to be honest had us a little bit over a barrel. Julie was due to give birth the next day and I didn't want to be away the other side of the county, working, in case anything happened.

That, given with the fact that due to Nick's deal, we had let other potential buyers go meant I was left with no choice. Besides, I trusted him.

"Sure, see you tomorrow." I agreed.

We shook hands and he left. The next day I woke early to the sounds of our van, now Nick's van, being driven out of the road. He had started his new business early, which seemed to be a good sign.

The day dragged as we waited for him to return with our money and this gave me a chance to think. We had agreed not to involve solicitors in the deal as we trusted each other but I decided I wanted something in writing and so drew up a contract of sale. He could read it and sign it later on when he handed over the cash.

Night-time approached and there was no sign of the baby, and judging by the look on Nick's face when he arrived at our door, no sign of the money either.

"Can you believe it?" he asked. "I put the car in dad's auction, and to boost the price up and he bid for it. The only thing is, he bid so high that nobody would match it. Don't worry though I am meeting a lad at 6 o'clock on Monday. He's having it instead."

I was starting to get fed up with the repeated excuses and lack of cash but I felt a bit easier when he signed the contract. In fact he didn't hesitate to do so.

"I need the money by Monday at the latest Nick," I told him.

"Of course," he said offering me his hand. "Don't worry. I'm good for it."

I could go on and bore you, the reader, with the details but I am sure you can guess what is coming and what happened next.

He made excuse after excuse after excuse at the lack of cash. A month went by and Julie had given us a lovely little boy who we named Cy Tyson. A new sparring partner for his sister.

However, still no money from Nick just more excuses. I called on him early on Thursday evening. One of his mates who lived at the house with him, a podgy little chap called Tony, answered the door.

"Oh, hi Si. There's a check for you here," he told me as he waddled back into the house.

At last! A check wasn't cash but it was better than nothing and was a sign of good intent. However, Tony came back to the door a minute later empty handed.

"I'm sorry, I can't find it," he grinned weakly.

"Look Tony, this is pissing me off! Tell Nick to come and see me when he gets back, I want this sorting out." I told him.

Tony just nodded and went back to sipping his beer. Up to this point, in a further effort to help Nick get the business going, we had continued to take the phone bookings from our office. A pattern was starting to emerge. We noticed Nick drinking more and more and the complaints being made from customers were coming in on a regular basis.

 He was ruining a business he had yet to pay a penny for. One Saturday morning we were flooded with calls. They ran along the lines of Nick not turning up for bookings to turning up drunk with a van full of lads.

Not the kind of children's entertainment you would hope for. One customer phoned me wanting to know Nick's address. He had failed to turn up for a party and let down about forty kids. The dad was understandably upset.

However, it was not my place to give out Nick's home address and judging by the tone of the guy's voice, this was wise. I could see seven years of hard work disappearing in a short month.

"Shall we ask him for the business back?" suggested Julie.

"No, he's wrecked it. Besides, I want my money. He's got it and he's just being pig headed about it. Let him sort it out!" I was starting to get really angry and left a message for him to call on me that night. I would be up all night waiting for him.

About ten o'clock he turned up. I knew from the start that we were going to row.

"I'm pissed off now Nick, I want my money!" I yelled at him.

"Look I'm trying it's just that…" he tried but I cut him off.

"You're not trying hard enough! I'm not fucking about now Nick, you are ruining the business. Well that's your lookout, but I want my money. I can't move with my gym idea and that means I'm losing income every day".

He nodded his agreement.

"I'll have two grand tomorrow and the rest by the end of the week. I promise."

"Listen," I offered, "Stay off the drink and work this business. Christ, we made a fortune out of it. Sort it out."

He listened as I told him what people were starting to say about him.

"Yeah, fair enough." With that he went, making arrangements for the cash to be delivered by the morning.

You know sometimes when you wake up and you just know it is going to be a shit shaped day? I rose early and went to get the post. And then I saw it. His note.

He didn't even have the courage to tell me face to face, but wrote a pathetic note. I still have it now, tucked away in a file with all the other evidence against him that we were later to acquire.

"Si, sorry but I pulling out of the deal," he wrote. "My dad and I don't want the business anymore. See you later. Sorry." Simple as that. They *didn't* want the business anymore. Pair of spoilt brats and arrogant arseholes.

I felt sick. What did it have to do with his Dad? Nick was like a ruined child, giving back a broken toy after playing with it for almost two months and taking a lot of money from it.

I immediately phoned my solicitor and explained our situation. He listened then offered his opinion. He told us we were wise to get the contract signed and that we were on safe ground with the sale. He also asked whether or not I believed Nick had the money, which I did. He suggested I write to Nick giving him a week to pay before we commenced legal action.

I sat down and drafted out the letter, which I then took to his house. His mate Tony grunted as he took it from me. I couldn't care less, he was an idiot anyway.

Later on that night there was the inevitable knock at the door. It was Nick.

"Si, can we talk?" he asked.

"There is nothing to say. You need to pay what you owe. Look, you've taken my business, ruined it and now want me to have it back. No chance! I've got commitments and a family to look after. Get me my money." I demanded.

"You can have it back, the business I mean. You could build it back up."

I couldn't believe the nerve of the man. I had worked hard for seven years, sacrificing many things, including a social life to work every weekend to make this business a success. He had ruined it in a few weeks and now I was supposed to bail him out? Not a hope in hell. I wanted what was mine.

"Listen, I want my money or we are going to go to court. I mean it, I'll ruin you Nick, I promise!"

His next words reinforced my resolve. Any slight chance of a back down on my part went up in smoke with his next words:

"You couldn't do that. You're too nice," were his famous last words.

Believe me, he wasn't paying me a compliment; he was saying he thought I was a mug.

"Get out of my house. Now," I said it quietly, putting a bit of menace in my voice.

He left and the next day, all legal and above board, High Court action was started against him.

To 'sum up' (if you will excuse the pun), the British legal system let me down. It stunk. I followed the law to the very letter and its first instructions were that that I had to have the summons served on him personally.

Fine, I wanted him to know how personal I was going to get. I wasn't going to hide behind process servers, I would do it myself.

One Saturday morning, after his usual all night booze up and loud music, upsetting all the nice people who live in our area, him and his ever-growing army were sleeping it off.

I felt nervous, knowing that the house was full of lads but so what. I was becoming friends with fear; it seemed we were to walk through this life hand in hand.

I banged the door as hard as I could. After sometime, Nick opened the door. Looking bleary eyed, stinking of booze and quite clearly hung over, he looked surprised to see me.

Ignoring the noise from the guys inside the house, I handed him the summons.

"Here, you've been served!"

"No thanks mate!" he laughed weakly as he tried to shut the door. I slammed my foot in it, stopping him, and threw the summons at him.

"See ya!" I laughed as I walked back to our house.

The summons required him to defend my action within thirty days or have judgment enforced on him. Same old Nick, above everything, he chose to ignore the summons.

It was a long thirty days, living next door to a house that was becoming increasingly more filled with thugs. He had started to attract the undesirables with his parties, boozing and late nights.

Bad looks, veiled threats were the order of the day until I told Julie to stop it!

Seriously, on the thirty first day, the court told us that no defence had been entered and we were awarded a High Court judgment. We gave him fourteen days to pay.

Again, Nick being Nick ignored everything and continued to party. It was now apparent that he was taking in something other than drink.

He still wouldn't pay up and so I called a bailiff in. Now don't get me wrong, if I had seen Nick penniless, working as hard as he could to get by, then I would have backed off and worked it out. I'm not an animal, but neither was I a mug anymore.

He was living in a house valued at about twice the value of other houses in the area. He had an array of cars at his disposal and was shifting more beer for him and his mates than you could wave a big stick at.

He was, in short, taking us for fools. The bailiff called to his house and was very easily put off by Nick's excuses.

"What, I owe Simon money?" he asked incredulously. "I don't know anything about this!"

"Well, that's not my problem, I have an order from the court to take your stuff," replied the bailiff.

"Well I don't own anything. Everything here belongs to my dad," he lied.

I couldn't believe what happened next. The bailiff just swallowed the complete story.

"I'll be back in two weeks and I want to see proof that this stuff is your dad's or I'm taking it," He told Nick. And with that he toddled off back to fairy tale land.

Ten minutes later, a neighbor phoned me at work. Nick's dad had turned up with a van and was emptying the house of any removable contents. Nice work if you can get it.

The only thing left was Nick's fancy white sports car, which he couldn't, or for sake of image, wouldn't hide. He then contacted a solicitor who went before the court and have our judgment overturned.

However, so the bailiff informed us, until the court hearing, goods could still be taken and so without further ado, after much pressure from me, he returned to the house, snatched Nick's fancy sports car and put up for sale. We felt things were beginning to turn in our favor.

The hearing to have the judgment set aside was set for January, but we were convinced we had done everything right and he would not be successful.

However, everyone makes mistakes, and I then made my biggest. For reasons I'm not sure I understand myself, I changed solicitors to attend the hearing. Communications went back and forth and Julie and I gave our new legal eagle our true version of accounts.

Then we were served with Nick's version, his 'defence'. I felt sick with rage and anger as I read it.

He claimed I had made the whole thing up and that I had actually forged his signature on the contract. Further, he claimed he had no money and had only been running the business to help us out during Julie's pregnancy.

I told my solicitor to inform the court that I was quite happy for the police to investigate the alleged forgery. I had nothing to fear or to hide. She told me it was best, for what reason I have no idea, to just let things run as they are and not to involve the police. I was also told I could not attend the Monday morning hearing, but I was sure justice would prevail and our Judgment would stand. I was wrong. The court, according to my lawyer, didn't believe anything Julie and I had said. They ordered judgment to be set aside for a full hearing, the car to be returned and me to pay all the legal costs.

When the phone call came through late afternoon I felt like crying. Other than stealing a pack of chewing gum from a local store when I was about ten, I have never stolen in my life. I don't do dishonesty, I just don't. Neither does Julie.

We believe in honesty, integrity and truth. It is a shame that we can't say the same for the British legal system. Believe me, I felt the full, unjustified force of it. I felt so low. His affidavit, sworn on oath, was a tissue of lies.

However, even worse than this, I was about to get the biggest kick in the balls of my life. He had told the court that he didn't have any money. Then, the following Wednesday, a guy I didn't know, visited me at one of my karate clubs. He had heard off my plight. It was the local gossip by now, and he had also heard that Nick was rubbing his hands at his victory and to celebrate was buying himself a new car.

The court had ordered that the car that the bailiff had snatched was to be returned and I was sent a bill for over £300.00 to deliver it back to Nick. Order of the court. Well they could fuck off, I wasn't paying it!

Now the car that was going to raise the money to pay for our business was to be used for a little run around for Nick's cronies.

Four days after he told the court that he had no money, Nick pulled up outside the house with a brand new top of the range, sports car. To rub salt into the wound, he left the price in the window, £37,950.00

He laughed when I drove past him toward home, as he was surrounded by his cronies admiring his new motor.

People started trying to egg me on. It was inevitable and obvious that some people, family included, thought they could 'handle' the situation better than me.

"We can have him sorted! It'll cost you but he won't be laughing then!" was a common 'war cry'.

Strangely enough, the people making the loudest noises were the people I had no faith in at all. They were 'plastic gangsters' who read too many books.

One guy chose a family party to inform me, rather loudly;

"He wouldn't live next door to me!"

"Why?" I asked bored with this constant taunting and bullshit.

"I'd be anonymously sending pizzas and taxis to his house all hours! That would keep him awake."

Fucking hell! Why didn't I think of that? This was the kind of action Al Capone built his empire on! I could just imagine Nick, "No, please, no anchovies, I'm allergic!"

I felt lost. I wanted to hurt the deceitful bastard but every time I the temptation grew strong, I would look at my children in bed. They stopped my heart with their smooth skin, big blue eyes and fantastic laughs. I looked at Julie. She was gorgeous. They relied on me, and I certainly relied on them. They were my life.

Being away from them would kill me. I could handle Nick, no problem at all. It was the thought of doing time for it that killed me. The scumbag just wasn't worth it.

Still, the wannabes continued. One person in particular seemed to enjoy telling me how to sort it, and seemed to enjoy my pain. In fact he seemed to revel in it. This hurt me the most because this person was the one I thought I could rely on the most. This was the one person who I thought would see I was choosing the right way to go about things. This person was my dad…

He would love to announce to anyone in ear shot that he would have this sorted overnight. These brags more often than not took place in my company, to my embarrassment and usually to the embarrassment of the people with us.

"Simon is doing this all wrong," he would advise, "I could make a phone call right now and this would be over. I'll get the ***** brothers out from Liverpool (this was a prominent crime family from 'over the water' who ran, amongst other things, the door security network in a city known for its hard cases).

Many years later, I would learn that this family, although doing business with my father, thought of him as a joke, despite his bragging to the world that he was 'connected' to them (this is covered in a lot more detail in my book, *'An Everyday Warrior'*).

However, this did not stop his constant bullshit and attempts at making himself look bigger by making me look smaller. He knew I adored my family and would not do anything that would jeopardize my liberty and take them away from me.

I tried reasoning with him, after he'd had a particularly good laugh at my expense in front of a gathering of work colleagues.

"Dad, who do you think the first person the Police are going to come to if anything happens to Nick? It is common knowledge of his debt to me and you are of course forgetting, his sister is quite high up in the Police force. Mine is the first door they will knock on."

He laughed and seemed to take pleasure in what he saw as my 'weakness'. I tried to explain even further.

"So, okay, we get him 'taken care of'. Maybe a beating or his legs broken. I then go away for at least three years. Now I don't know if you have noticed, but we live right next door to him, so whilst I am locked up, Julie and the kids have to live right next door to the guy whose legs are now in plaster, but who is still surrounded by thugs and violent people Who is going to look after them, to protect them? You?"

He still didn't get it and one night, after a session drinking, he told me, to show off in front of his friends that he would 'buy the debt off me.'

"What do you mean?" I asked.

"Well, you are owed £17,000. I buy the debt on paper. We say I have bought it off you for £2,000 and the money is owed to me. I'll put a couple of 'the boys' in and we give them £2,000 for their troubles when we get the money."

I knew him to be full of the brown stuff, he just wanted the debt in his name to look big in front of his mates, who by now, were cringing and obviously felt for me. They too were tired of his nonsense.

By now I had also had quite enough of him and so decided to surprise the life out of him. To call his bluff:

"That's a great idea dad," I agreed. "You give me £2,000 tomorrow and then what you collect is yours."

He gasped and spilt his pint. "Don't be stupid. I'm not going to give you £2,000. It is just a plan to get your money."

I nodded, pretending to go along with it all.

"Right, I see. So will we definitely get the money?" I asked.

"Oh yes. These guys don't take no for an answer," he bragged.

"So if you give me the "£2000 yourself and pay them £2,000, you will still walk away with £13,000. That's a lot of money for putting your name to something. I'm happy with £2,000 so we all win. It's a no lose situation." I enjoyed seeing him squirm, I was sick of his big man crap.

His friends looked on interested and amused.

"Simon has a point there Peter. Take him up on it." one suggested.

"No, no, no. You don't understand. What it is …"

I cut him off. "No. You said it was easy. You will collect all that money, no hassle no questions. I get something back and no police are involved. If you are that confident that your 'boys' will do this for you then I don't see the problem."

He was furious! He could barely speak to me and then came the inevitable:

"Right, I'm calling a taxi. I'm off home. Come on Julie (my mum) we are going." He then turned to me and in a spiteful way told me, "You will *never* get your money!"

"No," I retorted "and neither will I end up in prison."

One of his friends winked at me and out of ear shot of my dad said this:

"Well done Si. Don't listen to him, he is full of shit. You are doing things the right way."

Still, you expect your dad to support you on this kind of thing, not join the ignorant masses calling for slaughter.

But still, he had put doubt in my head. Was I a coward again? I didn't fear Nick. Well not in any special way, just the fear that we all feel in any confrontation. I could take him, I knew I could. What should I do?

To answer another friend who was singing from the same hymn sheet as my dad (and also couldn't 'fight sleep') I put this to him:

"You have a daughter yes?" I asked, knowing the answer. He nodded, not sure of where this was going.

"To date, with costs, Nick owes me almost £17,000. If I were to give you that amount, would you agree not to see your daughter for a few years. During those few years you have to live in an eight foot by eight foot box. Oh, and while you are there, your wife and children have to live right next door to the reason you are in prison in the first place."

I give this man his due, he thought about it quietly and then nodded.

"Yeah, put like that, who cares about the money?"

Some weeks later, when another "gangster" put in his opinion, my friend jumped on him. "You haven't got a clue mate. What does Simon want to go to prison for? At the end of the day it's just money. Look at his family, he'd lose them in a second."

I admired him for this, for now he understood.

Still pressure mounted up from all sides. Financially, we were being crippled. Our dream of a gym was over. I continued to work in the factory and every time I drove home and into our driveway, it seemed Nick had even more lads at his house, all trying their best to intimidate me. All failed miserably.

And then the good side of conflict emerged. An old personal friend of mine, a former professional heavyweight boxer and head doorman of lots of local nightclubs, heard of my plight. He arranged a meeting.

"Brilliant!" I thought miserably, "now he's going to give me his thoughts on life."

He did indeed offer me his thought and advice. I was surprised, but then realized knowing the man that I shouldn't have been.

"Don't do anything silly about this, Simon, do it legal," he said quietly and sagely.

"What!?" I didn't expect this.

"I've done prison, Si. It's shit. Three years away from your wife and children. Do it legal. If you want him to get a smack, well…that's up to you but the legal way is best. At the end of the day, it's just money. Don't do time for no one."

I already had a healthy respect for this giant, mainly due from the hard hitting punches I took from him during our regular one on one boxing sessions together. But this put him in a whole new light.

He was hard, no doubt about it, but his view of my situation put other "hards" to shame. I shook his hand.

"Thanks," I simply told him. "Thanks."

"No problem, anytime. And if things get rough, well then that's different. Keeping you out of prison is one thing, but keeping you and your family safe, well. Don't let this arsehole and his lot try and hurt anyone. Don't show them any fear, Simon. Not one bit. You have my number, you know where I am."

I was beginning to get it. It was from people like this that I learnt the stuff I thought years of training would teach me. The Martial Arts gave me the courage to deal with the situation, but I was going to have to alter my view of things.

In the meantime, Nick was surrounding himself more and more with thugs. This gave me, strangely enough, a bit of comfort. If he wasn't scared, then why would he have these Muppets around?

But I had to do more. My main priority was my family. I needed to keep them safe and stay inside the law. Physical was out of the question. I had to take him to a higher plain, the mental psych out. Scare him enough to make sure his bunch of goons stayed away from Julie and the kids. I didn't want anybody trying to scare us away from this case. Things were about to get interesting.

CHAPTER ELEVEN

I decided I would bide my time and beat Nick at mind games. After all, he was starting to show signs of limited intelligence by the crowd he was hanging about with. It wouldn't be hard to beat him at this and I wouldn't have to wait long.

For my money, if somebody swears on oath, something that is not true, then they have committed perjury. I don't have a brilliant legal mind, but I know right from wrong and I believed our authorities did to. Apparently I was wrong.

I contacted the police and informed them that I had, by all accounts, committed forgery on a business deal worth a lot of money. This was a matter of record as in Nick's sworn statement that he said he had not signed the contract. He claimed I had done it for him. They (the police) should investigate me.

"Sorry," they told me "We are not interested."

I then informed them that I had evidence of perjury. All they had to do was run a forensic check on Nick's signature, * establish that it was indeed his, read his sworn affidavit claiming he had never signed or indeed even seen the contract and there you have it.

*At a later date, West Midlands Police did indeed run forensic tests on the documents in question. It came back 'positive' that it was Nick's signature yet still no prosecutions were brought against him for perjury, despite the tests being backed up by a copy of his affidavit.

"Sorry," they again informed me. "We aren't interested. It is a civil matter."

I then made a complaint against Nick: I claimed he received goods by false pretences.

"What are the false pretences?" they asked me.

"The fact that he led me to believe he had the money to buy my business and apparently, he doesn't."

"Well he might have the money," they argued.

"But it says in his SWORN affidavit, that he doesn't." I relayed.

"Well maybe he hasn't got it then," was their comeback.

"But he led me to believe he had. That is surely false pretences."

"We don't know what's in his mind, do we? Sorry, we're still not interested."

Was I not getting the bigger picture here?

So I went it alone. If the authorities weren't interested then there was no need for Nick to know that. Bluff was called for.

My opportunity came quick. I was driving home one night when I spotted his big flash sports car driving along a busy main road. Sitting in it was Nick and one of his hired guns. I did a 'U' turn and followed them to a local supermarket. Waiting until his passenger went into the shop, I drove up and blocked Nick in as he tried to turn his car around.

He had his stereo booming and was trying to look cool but didn't hide his fear very well. I did. Years of being partners with fear and recent successes in dealing with it had taught me how to hide it well. As I approached him on foot, he wound down his window.

"What?" he tried to spit out. I laughed at his attempt at 'hard'. I had spent many an hour in the company of hard men, usually in the ring or on the mats swapping blows. Yes, I had seen hard and he wasn't it.

"You're a thief and a con man. A spineless one at that," I said menacingly but quietly, not wanting draw attention to us.

"Look Si, please mate, let's sort this out," he pleaded.

"I'm not your mate, but yeah, we can sort this out. Pay me my fucking money!"

"I haven't got it, honest," he cried out.

I couldn't believe what I was hearing. He was sat in a car worth more than some people spend in a lifetime.

"You haven't got any money! Look at your fucking car!"

"Do you think this is paid for?" he asked, pitifully.

"What, it isn't? You ripped the garage off as well!? Tell you what, do you know what perjury is? It's when you lie on oath. You lied on oath. You committed perjury. At the end of all this, you're doing three years inside! I've already spoken to the police about it," I bluffed.

I had no idea whether he would or wouldn't eventually go to prison but then neither did he.

At this point his monkey came back from the shop. I shot him a look.

"This has fuck all to do with you! Stay away!" I shouted.

He hesitated and then developed an unhealthy interest in a nearby wall, inspecting it at close range. It can make you do funny things, fear.

I laughed at them both, got back in my car back and went home.

Round one to me.

But it wasn't going to be that easy. No, things were going to get much tougher. We had always enjoyed our Sundays. The kids played whilst we listened to music, usually Bruce Springsteen or Suzzane Vega, and had a nice glass of wine and enjoyed each other's company.

Then our Sunday peace was shattered. Julie was in the kitchen when she called out to me:

"Si, you better come and look at this." I could hear the tension in her voice and so was apprehensive as I went to her. She pointed out of the window at Nick's house. There were about four cars parked alongside his front garden. Approaching these cars, coming from the inside of his house was a gang of lads, about ten in all. They looked like they had just woken up after a heavy Saturday night.

Obviously, they had been partying the night away at Nick's and were now making their way home. They also thought they were tough and some of them looked it.

One in particular had the strangest haircut I had ever seen, sort of shaved and spiky at the same time. He also wore a black bomber jacket sporting the name of a local door security firm.

Apparently he was a bouncer at a rave club and a known drug dealer. He also had the largest Rottweiler I had ever seen, walking by his side. Nick looked like the cat that had got the cream with his new "security".

I shrugged and laughed to show Julie I wasn't concerned, trying not to worry her. Homework had to be done on this lot.

The following Tuesday I went to see my boxer friend who had kindly given me the advice about staying out of prison and explained, or rather described, what and who I had seen. He knew them all, including "haircut".

"He's a prick, Simon. Nothing to worry about." he told me.

The thing is, when you are an eighteen stone ex professional boxer with a sledgehammer punch not many people are a worry to you. I told him this and he smiled.

"No Simon. You'" he motioned to me, "have nothing to worry about. Catch him with one of your kicks and he is going down, without a doubt."

I was, perhaps rather immaturely, flattered. I had sparred many rounds of boxing with this man and considered him very tough. The respect he gave me back through this comment boosted my confidence.

I remember still, the fear I used to feel making the twice-weekly trips to his house, where we used to train together in his gym. We would warm up on the bags and then get into eight or nine rounds of boxing. He was tough, no doubt about it, and on more than one occasion, I would leave his house with my head ringing from the punches he had dished out. I was also, secretly pleased, that my newfound courage enabled me to go back for more and try and give as good as I got.

If I had the bottle for that, then the Mickey Mouse crew next door would not bother me. Well, not that they would see anyway.

The pattern continued with the house next door slowly becoming the focal point for the area's scum and drug users. Neighbors were in despair, but Nick didn't give a shit. He was having the ride of his life. Well I was about to start making his ride a bit more uncomfortable.

Every time I saw him, I would hold up three fingers and inform him:

"Three years mate! That's what you get for perjury. Three years when this is over!" I would then laugh at the sickly look that came over him.

It was different when he was with his friends though. He would grin like the big hero, as they laughed and egged him on.

"Laugh all you like mate, prison isn't so funny," I would say, never letting him get the last word. Deep down I knew he was terrified.

Given the lifestyle, characters at the house and nightly comings and goings, it was now becoming obvious he had completely gone over to the dark side and was dealing drugs from his house.

We decided to try and obtain some kind of evidence on Nick. Something we could use to help our case and to finish his dealings, to finish him. Be it photos of him actually in possession of the assets of our business, or some proof of his ever-growing drug involvement.

We enlisted the services of a private detective that promised us the earth, all for the princely sum of £150. After parting with a cheque for half up front, we sat back and waited for the results.

A couple of weeks went by before I received a phone call from him.

"Do you have good security?" he asked.

"Why, what's up?" I replied.

"I've looked into him and his family. Apparently they are nasty and into revenge attacks. Just be careful. It may be worth your while trying to settle this."

Not a chance. I would not be bullied anymore. I had to let Nick know that on a level he would understand. My chance, thankfully, came sooner rather than later.

It was a hot Saturday afternoon and I was enjoying a sit down in the front garden when Nick pulled up in his flash car. He got out and at his side was a girl of no more than sixteen.

What had happened to this guy? Less than a year previously, he had been sunning himself in Florida with his partner, Alison, and little boy, Tim. She was a very pretty girl at twenty six and had a good job at a bank. Nick was popular with the local people and his life was going places.

Then he turned bandit. Alison had long since gone, taking with her the little boy. Now here he Nick, going nowhere fast, keeping kids for company. He was in his thirties for God's sake!

He was losing weight from the parties and wild life and couldn't see that he was being a idiot. No, he thought he was king of the hill, with his band of merry men.

He walked toward the front of the house, trying to look hard. I held up my three fingers.

"Three years . Three years in prison!" I motioned to the girl, "She'll be old enough to walk home from school on her own by the time you get out!" I kept my fingers up.

"You'll get them fingers cut off one day," he muttered. I jumped from the chair and threw my sunglasses down.

"What did you fucking say!" I screamed.

He turned his sickly color again and whilst trying to get his key in the front door muttered, "I just said, you know, your fingers..." He stammered as his girl looked on confused and a bit embarrassed.

"I'll tell you what, hang on there, I'll go and get my samurai sword and hold my fingers up for you. You can cut them off if you want." I was hyper and could see he was not comfortable at all. In fact he looked terrified.

"Look Si…"

"Look Si nothing!" I cut him dead "You are not f***ing good enough to even try. Nor is anyone you know!"

He looked a bit shocked, as if he knew what I was referring to, as if he knew the detective had warned me off. He turned and walked away toward the back door and a quicker entrance to his house. Well maybe not quicker, but at least at the back door he didn't have me screaming at him.

I laughed as he scurried away. I was getting good at this! At this time, another event, looming on the horizon, was bringing its own form of stress. Geoff Thompson had invited me to his Coventry Real Fight Academy to take my 2nd Dan. I had a while to go but knew it was going to be very tough and had started training for it already.

To my further delight, Geoff and his lovely wife Sharon had agreed to stand as our little boy's Godparents. Julie and I were thrilled when they made the trip up from the Midlands to the christening. It would be a welcome break from the anxiety of living next door to hell.

I was suffering a bit and starting to feel the pressure. Nick's house was now a proper den of iniquity and was full of gangs of drunk, high lads. The simple act of going out of the front door, to the car in the morning, or driving home having to go past the house was becoming tiresome and stressful.

As part of my training, I would go out running a couple of times a week, but the whole run would be dominated by the thought that I would have to run past his house to get home and there was always the chance that a "team" would be outside.

They may be outside drinking, or I could just run into them by accident as they made their way to their cars. Either way, the pressure of facing them was hard. I would force myself to run harder and be more determined, but one of the most difficult things in the world is to run toward the danger whilst your instincts are telling you to run away from it.

Still, I would not let them stop my training, despite some of the incidents we were now hearing about. A friend had told us that he had been into the house and had seen some of the lads with heroin. Another person told us of a horrific incident when someone in the house had had a thousand pounds stolen from them. The lads in the house took to the suspected culprit with an electric cattle prod and beat him senseless.

This was the kind of thing we were living next door to, this is the kind of scum we were up against. The constant threat of violence hung in the air.

So a good christening, a good family party away from all this was just what we needed. Our families gathered at my parents' house and it was here I was to get the strangest talk I have ever had.

Geoff could see that I was a bit low and took me to one side to talk to me.

"This guy next door, it worries you doesn't it?" he asked.

"Yeah, of course," I responded.

"Don't let it, Simon. It's a gift," he said, gently.

I thought for a second I had misheard him and he had said "he's a git". I couldn't argue with that. But no, I hadn't heard him wrong.

"How can something this bad be a gift Geoff? It's terrible. We don't deserve this. Not just the money, but the bloody lifestyle next door and the constant threatening atmosphere."

"Believe me Simon. You need this. You'll get through it and be really strong for it. You'll look back at this in a year and be proud of yourself for the way you are handling it. It will make your training better, your teaching better and people will listen to you. Just treat it like a gift." He is a very wise man is Mister Thompson.

"People keep telling me to give him a smack or get him beaten up. It's easy enough to do." I offered miserably.

"It's not the answer Simon. It's the easy way out. You're doing fine. If anything happens to him, who is the first person the police will think of? Really, you've got too much to lose."

This was another surprise. Between Geoff and my friend the ex boxer, they were probably the two toughest men I knew and yet both of them denounced the violence that could cost me prison.

I couldn't have enough respect for these two friends, and considered myself very lucky that I could call them that.

"Don't lose your liberty for a lemon!" Geoff told me. He was telling me what I already knew, but I just needed reassuring.

I would continue handling the situation the same way. I would not be threatened, I certainly wouldn't let my family be threatened but I would carry on with my aggressive manner towards the thugs next door.

They must know in no uncertain terms that if they were to go too far, I would punish them. They had to be scared of me and perhaps think I was a loose canon.

I had a great opportunity to show Nick I was "not quite right", and though it seems nothing now, I know at the time it put the fear of God into him.

Winter had arrived with a vengeance and the court case seemed nowhere near. One horrible November night gave me my chance to prove I had a 'screw lose'.

I had just got out the bath and had only a pair of shorts on. Outside the wind was terrific and hammered the rain against our windows. Julie was in the kitchen only this time, her voice had my heart pounding with excitement.

"Si, Nick's at his front door. I think he's going out!"

I looked and saw him wrapped up in a heavy coat and woollen hat. It was freezing, too cold for anyone else to be out. Wearing only my shorts, I knew I had to be quick.

I ran outside to the front garden, and stood in the middle of the mud. Nick left his door and walked toward his car.

"Hey, dickhead! Three years if I don't get my money!" I shouted to him.

He jumped out of his skin. Turning to face me I could see what he was thinking. It looked to him like I was just stood in the front garden, in my shorts, in a gale, for the fun of it. He hadn't seen me run from the front door and as far as he knew, I had been enjoying the weather for ages.

He didn't know what to do and looked even more worried when I started making chicken noises and flapping my arms like wings.

He turned and scurried back to his house, slamming the door shut behind him. He had decided against going about his business and obviously thought I had gone mad.

Good, who wants to fight a mad man? I waited a couple of seconds, then legged it back to the warmth of the house were Julie stood, laughing at me.

"Bloody hell Ju, it's freezing out there. Make us a cup of tea love!"

It seemed that every time some of Nick's gang got the message and gave up trying to be threatening toward us, he would replace them with another batch of toughs.

The road became a hazard as they sped up and down in their high performance cars. Sitting by the window one night, a couldn't help but notice a white sports car screeching past our house, the driver looking in our window laughing. I was up and out of the door in a flash.

"Oi! Come here!" I ordered him.

He looked surprised. Obviously this wasn't part of the plan. Nick had obviously told him he could pretty much do what he wanted to wind me up. I wouldn't give him any trouble.

Wrong answer.

His eyes darted in the direction of Nick's door, looking for any backup. There was none. It was just me and him. He didn't like his odds much.

"Yes mate, what is it?" he said, meekly.

"First, I'm not you mate. Secondly, fucking pack in driving past my house like that!" I ordered, not requested.

"Listen, mate." He cut his sentence short, obviously getting the message that I was not his 'mate' "I'm not getting involved in your argument with Nick. I don't want to get into it with you…"

"No you don't!" I interrupted

"Well I'm only hanging around 'cause he owes me money," he sniveled.

"I'm not interested. Pack in that driving and stopped trying to act hard. Cos' you're not". I told him.

He nodded, "Fair enough, sorry." He offered me his hand.

Two weeks later he left Nick's house never to be seen again.

Still the stress seemed to pour on. I was now weeks away from taking my 2nd Dan and knew I was in for a hard time trying to get it.

I was running, sparring, doing heavy bag work and weight training. The training, it would seem, was beginning to pay off.

At a club session one Friday evening, I arranged for three of my senior students to stay behind for a full contact sparring session. It was all voluntary, and because of the nature of the training I would not force anybody to do it.

They had to feel the fear of full contact fighting, and get past that fear themselves. If you try and force people to train in this way, you run the risk of resentment and lack of progress. Because the person fighting doesn't want to fight, they will not perform to the best of their ability which leads to them getting hurt.

I knew that I would face a massive task in Coventry and really wanted to be put under pressure. My thinking was that if all my people would fight two, three minute rounds each against me, rotating after each round, then I would be fighting fresh people all the while.

I would allow myself only the time it took to change opponents for my rest and when the sparring was done, we would take the mitts of and repeat the format on the ground, wrestling with chokes, strangles and locks until one or the other submitted.

I told the fighters, so they would be under no false illusions that the idea was to try and knock each other out. This wasn't going to be an easy session and they should be prepared for it.

The usual suspects, my higher graded people put their hands up to take part and a few more nervously followed. In all a total of six opponents were "up for it" and we arranged to meet the following Friday.

My nerves where in overdrive for the whole week and on the day of the session the niggling doubt set in. Could I keep the pace up against six fresh faces? Being as I was only slim, they were all heavier than me, and at fifteen stone, weight trainer Stuart was almost half my weight again.

"No," I countered myself, "I'm more than ready for this. I'm fit, strong and have been at this for some time. I know this will be tough but I've got to do it."

I willed myself into a positive state of mind, reminding myself that I had done many rounds of full contact and lot of floor fighting. Never against six fresh people but there is always a first.

I arrived at the sports centre, and as I thought, some people had bottled it. I don't know why, they had all sparred full contact before, but maybe it was the format which made them feel extra pressure. I wasn't angry with them. Your bottle goes, it happens. It had happened to me when I was younger more times than I care to count. I just hoped they were able to get over it.

Still, the three that had turned up were the most advanced members of the club anyway and I had expected that they would be there.

"Right lads, here's how it works" I addressed them. "We are going to try and knock each other out, yes?"

They nodded their agreement.

"If you get the chance, do it to me because I am certainly going to do it to you should you stick your chin out. I don't care in what order you come, just make sure you're gloved up and ready when it's your turn. I don't want any breaks or chances to stop, okay? Because we have three no shows, I need you to do more rounds than we expected."

My adrenalin was sky high as they sorted themselves out, but I knew I hid it well.

Stuart looked massive as he pulled his gloves on, put his gumshield in and turned to face me.

"Touch gloves and fight," ordered Chris, our third party supervisor (there was no need for a referee) and off we went.

Stuart threw a long jab which I felt the full force of. Shrugging it off I threw my own fast and hard combinations, everyone hitting their target which was the centre of his face.

He was big but couldn't match my speed and tried to back-pedal. I followed him and kept throwing punch after punch after punch. He started to turn his back and I leaned around him and banged him on the temple.

"No that's enough, sorry." He turned away, very distressed. I couldn't believe it. About one minute had gone by.

"Sorry Si," he offered, a bit embarrassed.

"Stuart, it's no problem, you tried and that's the main thing." I touched his gloves as Chris moved toward me to take his turn.

He also threw a good couple of punches and attempted to sweep my legs. I avoided it and caught him with a low thigh kick. As he wobbled I hook punched him in the head and he went down.

To his credit he was right back up and came after me. The fight went on for a minute or so more when I started combination punching again. Chris dropped to the floor and fell onto his front. I turned him on to his side, and he spat his gumshield out, breathing heavily.

"Alright mate?" I asked him concerned.

"Yeah, give us a minute will you?" he said, trying to catch his breath and his senses.

After a few seconds he stood on wobbly legs. There would be no more for him tonight.

Pete looked apprehensive as he took his turn on the mats. After some more aggressive punching he too refused to continue and the room was subdued as we took our gloves off.

"Thanks lads," I offered.

"Well, it didn't last long did it?" one of them replied.

"It doesn't matter. I really appreciate your efforts, thanks."

I shook hands with them all and took them for a pint, but felt strangely disappointed by the events. I wanted a good hard session and got about four minutes of sparring. I should have been over the moon by my performance but I knew, with the greatest respect to the lads who had turned up for me, that Coventry would be a different league altogether.

I really did have a load of admiration for my lads but in Coventry, I was about to find out the difference between club class and world class.

In the aftermath of this session and about two weeks before my trip to Coventry, I received a very strange phone call. Now I had never told anybody about the sparring session, it is not my thing to brag. But a former student, a Scottish guy and 'story teller' who liked to talk a good fight but very rarely trained, citing one excuse or another, called me up.

"Hi Simon it's Derek," he announced in his strong Glaswegian accent.

"Oh, long time no see Derek." I replied, surprised to hear from him

"Yeah I've been working so I haven't had time to train," came his usual attempt at a believable excuse.

"What for a whole year?" I asked.

"Listen, I want to book some private lessons," he informed me. I had heard all this before from him and to be honest was getting a bit bored with it and his "no shows".

"Yes, no problem, fifteen pounds an hour. When do you want to do them?" knowing I was going to hear more lame reasons for why he couldn't train.

"Well I've got a bad leg so when that gets better will be best."

"No problem Derek, when you're ready gives us a ring and we will sort it out. Listen, it was nice to talk to you again," trying to get away before he bored the pants off me.

"Yeah, er, listen is it right you knocked out three of your men in one night?" he got in, before I could escape.

Chinese whispers had started.

"Not exactly, Derek. No." I didn't particularly want to go into it.

"What happened then?" he persisted.

"Well, when I see you on your private session, I'll tell you all about it." I knew he was never going to book a lesson and so this saved me having to relay the whole episode to someone who never trained anyway.

"Go on, tell us now."

"No, give us a call when your leg is better, send us your money and I'll book you in. Anyway mate, good to talk to you and see you soon," I retorted.

"Oh, okay then. See you." He got the message and hung up the phone sounding slightly disappointed.

Now I didn't want to be rude. I know some very kind people have been kind enough to take the time to talk to me over the years, but I didn't want to waste an hour on the phone, gossiping about what had happened.

I also knew that he had no intention of training. He just wanted a 'war story' to tell his mates over a few pints, something to get his teeth into:

"Oh yeah, Simon knocked out these three blokes," which is not exactly true, but close. "Yeah, he's a great mate of mine you know," which is not even exactly close.

Well he wasn't getting any juicy bits from me. I'll talk to anybody but about something worth talking about and if someone needs my help and I can give it, then they can have bucket loads of it.

But I like to train and do my talking where it counts, on the mats. I'm not about to sound off to someone who I'd never hear from again.

Guess what? I never heard from him again.

However, whilst all this was going on, things continued with the neighbors from hell. I continued to train every night and the beauty of all this was that most if it took place in my makeshift gym in my garage. This had the added benefit of intimidating, or certainly, nullifying any attempts the gang next door may make to either intimidate or threaten me.

At this time, they were dealing drugs on a heavy, regular basis. Friday and Saturday nights saw cars full of teens pull up outside Nick's door, one of them would go to the door and return to the car some seconds later, with something in their hand.

Why didn't the police act on the obvious dealings? Well, I think I know why, but this is not the time or place to say. That's a story for another time, and it would make very interesting reading indeed! Suffice to say that later on a complaint was made to North Wales Police about one of their officers and their conduct in this matter.

However, as for the gang, being brave on a pedestal of drugs is not the same as facing a person sober, especially when that person you are facing, is training seven days a week to fight and is particularly keyed up for a major up and coming fight/test.

I would laugh and score a small victory every time I went to train. It was summer again and the lot next door loved their barbecues.

However, they would pack up rapidly and head indoors once I started to train. I would have my music full blast and the extra adrenaline they gave me would be taken out on the punch bags.

In-between rounds, I would take my rest sitting on the shared fence, laughing at them cooped up in the house in the lovely warm weather. When I had finished and gone for my shower, they came back out again to enjoy their burgers and kebabs.

If I am making it sound easy, it wasn't. Financially we were crippled. Emotionally we were starting to fall apart. I was still controlling next door but it was taking its toll.

Then one night I nearly blew it and almost attacked Nick. It took all my self-control to stay inside, and it was all over something as silly as a kebab.

Costs in the case were now spiraling. In total he owed us almost £22,000. We were counting the pennies and treats were not forthcoming.

On this particular night, Julie had gone to bed early and I sat alone in the front room. I was starving and really fancied a takeaway but there was no money for one so I decided to make some toast. Whilst I was sat in the kitchen waiting for it, Nick's car pulled up and him and a friend got out.

I was seething at what I saw. The friend was carrying a box of beer and Nick had two big bags of food from the local kebab house. This bastard owed me a fortune, I was starving and didn't have the price of a bag of chips and he was feeding a bunch of druggies!

I forced myself to stay in control. "Stuff him! He needs the nourishment more than me!" I told myself. I left my toast, now feeling sick with anger, and went to bed. Proper sulking!

A few weeks went by and things had gone a little bit quiet between us, so Nick, being Nick, decided to push his luck. He knew that one of the things that would wind me up, would be to he parked his works van outside our window. So this is what he did, one Thursday night.

That's fine, I thought. I knew that later on that night he would want to go to work in it. So I took my car and blocked him in. Now he can't go anywhere and his work will suffer. We waited for him to knock at the door anticipating the fun I would have with him. This was going to be a laugh.

After a couple of glasses of wine, we retired for an early night, but I was surprised that no one had been to see us about the van. Then, about eleven o'clock there was a hammering on the door.

"This should be good," I laughed to Julie as I picked up the intercom.

"Yeah?" I asked.

I was surprised at the response: "It's the police, can you open the door?"

"What for?" I asked.

"You know what for, come on Mr Morrell open up".

I grinned as I let him in. Julie came to join us.

"Your car is blocking him in," he said, his observation being fine.

"What, the drug dealer next door has the nerve to call you. Why didn't he come himself?"

"He doesn't want any trouble and I don't know anything about drug deals."

And so the poor man got everything. We told him the lot. After an hour of listening to Julie and I pour our hearts out to him about how we got ripped off, he lost the will to live. With perfect timing, our baby started to cry, seemingly adding to our misery.

"He's not been well," Julie told the policeman. I thought for a minute he was going to give us the money himself!

"Look, I'm sorry for you troubles, I really I'm, but you have got to move your car," he informed me.

"Sorry, I can't. I've had a drink or two." I laughed inside as I told him.

"Well no one will know," he conspired with me.

"What? You are telling me, as a police officer, to drink and drive."

We both knew this was a big wind up but I was having a buzz.

"Alright then, I'll breathalyse you and if you're under the limit, you can move it."

"You can't breathalyse me for having a drink in my own house!" I said, laughing.

"Well I'll move it then!" he was getting annoyed.

"How do I know your insured? It's an offence to drive uninsured you know?"

"I'm a police officer, of course I'm insured!"

"Have you got your policy for me then?"

He just laughed, conceding defeat. "He," he motioned next door "is going to work at two o'clock this morning. I'm coming back then, and if you haven't moved your car, I'm going to arrest you."

"For what?" I asked, incredulously.

"Obstructing a public highway."

"You can't do that," I replied.

"Why not?" he asked, exasperated.

"Because this road is still owned by the builders. The council hasn't adopted it yet, so it's not a public highway. It's private property, I'm not committing an offence, I'm not moving anything!" I countered. He shook my hand and laughed. Fair play to him.

"You know your stuff son," he said laughing.

"I have to, living next door to this."

He nodded, "Good luck lad!" and with that he went.

The van was still blocked in ten hours later and was only set free when I went to work. A small victory but a victory nonetheless.

Fair enough I suppose, they decided to have a go back. I had been in from training about ten minutes one Friday night and next door was surprisingly quiet. From our back garden, locked away in their run, my two dogs started kicking off an enormous row. I ran to the patio window to see what the fuss was and was confronted by the hugest dog in the world that was butting the window, snarling at me. It was the Rottweiler from next door and looked like he was going to join us inside at any minute.

I grabbed my trustee samurai sword and opening the door slowly, screamed at it and swung for it. There was no way it was coming in; its intentions did not look honorable.

It backed up slightly but continued to make aggressive noises. I could hear laughing from next door and realized they had let the dog out on purpose. My own dogs were locked up but were trying to hurl themselves through the fencing to get at their dog.

The Rottweiler backed up further and I let him. I'm not that daft or brave that I am going to follow it! It suddenly turned on its heels and ran back next door as its owner whistled him. The rest of his little pack (the owner's) were snickering which left me fuming.

I knew that the house next door was full of thugs, probably high on substances, and I also knew that any visit by me would result in violence and a police visit.

If I had gone to them, I would be the one to bear the brunt of any police action. So I decided to throw the ball in their court, and insult the gangs' collective manhood.

I phoned them and could just imagine all of them sitting there, high, laughing and feeling brave. The answerphone picked up my call but I knew they would be listening via the speaker.

"Pick up the phone you shithouse!" I ordered.

Surprisingly, Nick did. "Yeah!" he said offering his toughest voice yet.

"You f***ing listen and you listen good. If that f***ing mutt comes near my house again I'll kill it and anyone that follows it! Do you understand?!" I screamed at him down the receiver.

"Don't tell me, tell the owner!" he replied smugly, his owner being Mr Haircut, drug dealing scumhead. I could hear them laughing as he handed over the phone.

"What?!" he barked (no pun intended) at me as he took the phone. I was going to have to be good to frighten this one. Or so I thought.

"You fucking prick! I've got a sword here that would cut down a tree and if your fucking beast comes anywhere near my property again, I'll chop the fucker in two! You as well if you want it!"

His response amazed me. I could feel the air whooshing from him as he realized he didn't have the stomach for this. Nick had not told him about this side of me. For him, this was just a laugh and a wind up at any easy victim. His bottle went completely, totally shocked by my vicious tone.

"Yeah, shit sorry, fair enough it won't happen again."

"It better not, if that dog goes near my wife or kids, you won't see it again! Do you understand me?!"

"Yeah, I'm sorry mate," he muttered.

I was surprised by his quick submission and put the phone down to explain what had happened to Julie, who was watching and listening with bated breath. The sword lay on the sofa next to me.

It was quiet for what seemed like ages, as I didn't speak for listening out for some sort of rumpus to arrive from next door. Minutes past and I was sure they would come for me mob handed. They didn't.

I told Julie what was said and half felt sorry for the guy until I got a look from Julie that told me not to. I never got trouble from haircut again and he went out of his way to be polite to me.

CHAPTER TWELVE

The pressure was starting to mount from the up and coming grading. I was training as hard as I could, whilst trying to deal with the pressure of the situation with next door. I felt I had nowhere to go from all the anxiety and was constantly in a state of fight or flight.

I would alternate between worrying about the grading and worrying about whether we could last the course with this gang of thugs until we got our court hearing. I would go to bed scared and wake up scared. It was a nightmare.

The grading was my choice. It was an effort to better myself, to further my career and to see exactly how far I could go and how much courage I had. The situation next door was not my choice. I was at the hands of another human being's lack of code, honor of integrity. I would be damned if I would let either of the situations beat me, dominate me or finish me off.

However, we would sometimes be lying in bed in the early hours of the morning and could hear the thumping of music from next door. Their pattern was sleep all day and party all night regardless of the people living around them and anyone who had work to do and a family to look after.

It was becoming increasingly harder not to involve the 'right type of people' to put a stop to this but I put such thoughts out of my mind and instead concentrated on my grading.

I started to watch some videos Geoff had sent me showing his lads in various fights. They were awesome. I knew soon that I was going to have to fight some full contact bouts with some of them.

I remember thinking, "For the love of God! Is there anymore pressure anybody out there would like to put on me? Please, this isn't enough pressure! I need more than the threat of drug dealing gangsters and the chance I may have my sense knocked out of me, on a day trip to Coventry!" Yes, I am sarcastic even under immense pressure.

We were sat one Sunday about three weeks before my grading and it got too much for me. I was well aware that not twenty yards away was a house full of thugs, pumped up with drink and drugs, who at any minute could explode into a hail of violence. There were the usual muscle cars parked out front, music blasting from inside and the high pitched screams of girls, doing God knows what and taking God knows what. Please may God help them.

My house was now secured with weapons strategically placed at all the right points and I was fitter, stronger and mentally tougher than I had ever been in my life.

It still didn't mean that I wasn't feeling it, but I sure as hell wasn't showing it. Not for anybody but Julie to see. We sat on the sofa and she gave me a cuddle and held my hand. Tears flowed (mine, not hers) and I couldn't say anything. I didn't have to, she just knew. She was my soulmate, my best friend and the person that knew everything about me, from my thoughts to my feelings. The more astute amongst you readers may now have gathered that I was starting to fall in love with her (sorry, couldn't resist a poor attempt at humor!) ☺

They say that it is dark before the light and this was the darkest I had ever been. I didn't know though how near, and how bright the light was going to be.

The trip to Coventry was a long one. I had started the morning throwing up caused by nerves and bullying myself (how ironic) into not backing down or 'bottling it'.

At every point I wanted to turn back and found it difficult to speak. I forced myself to focus and consoled myself with the fact that not many people make it this far. I knew today was the day I fought the monsters. Geoff's lads had a fearsome reputation and I was going to experience first-hand what it was like to be on the mats with them, throw hands with them and feel their force.

We arrived in Coventry and were met by two of Geoff's lads who took us to Coventry Boy's Club where the grading would take place.

When we got there, there were five of Geoff's fighters waiting. They are animals on the mat and gentlemen off it. These lads treated me like a superstar. When I opened the boot of my car they leaned in to carry my bags.

"No, no need for that!" I said embarrassed.

"Not at all, go on get inside, we'll get these for you," I was told by Matthew. Doors were held open for us and I was pointed in the direction of the changing rooms. They shook hands with Julie and took her to the room where we would fight, (me and them, not me and Julie. Sorry another bad humorous attempt☺) The room was a large second floor matted area.

"Geoff will be here soon," I was told.

I nodded and didn't mind the wait. Geoff had already told me that he was filming a video for a major magazine that day, so the fact that he took time out for me was a major honor.

Justin, a current European All Out fighting Champion (now known fashionably as Ultimate Fighting) offered to help me warm up with a roll around the mats and grappling fight. Jesus, warm up! I was knackered at the end of it, he was so strong.

Other lads offered encouragement and advice and I loved them for it. God knows I needed it. After about half an hour, Geoff arrived and immediately came over and hugged me.

"Are you okay?" he asked.

"Yes, just nervous." Inside I was shaking but didn't even want Geoff to see it. Geoff took a training session first and put everybody through some grappling drills. I was flattered and had my confidence boosted when Justin commented on my strength on the ground. This was followed by Geoff rubbing my shoulders and offering a similar compliment.

These guys do not offer them lightly or to flatter. They mean what they say and I knew this at the time which gave me a hell of a lift.

We then got onto the submission wrestling drills and the strength and ability of these lads was fantastic. I managed to get one submission but lost almost every other fight. Just when it seemed I had a decent choke or lock on one of them, they would roll out of it to place a submission hold on me. I take my hat off to them.

I have seen many good fighters, from Traditional Karate, Boxing, Kickboxing and most of the other combat sports. I have also fought and beaten many good fighters from the same sports but these guys where in a different league. I couldn't get near them.

After about half an hour of grappling, my muscles felt like they were on fire. I still had to do the full contact kickboxing fights and go through full contact punch and kick drills on the focus pads.

After my pad work was finished I grabbed a quick drink and it was time for the fighting. Two fighters, Justin and Lee were told to put their pads on and everybody else left the room to get a drink. Now, I'll share a secret here. I had watched Justin fight in the videos Geoff had sent me and was in awe of him. I had been praying that he wouldn't be one of my opponents so when he was told to stay, I very nearly bottled it.

However, I didn't and listened as Geoff gave me a pep talk in which he told me that I would have to earn my 2nd Dan and not just get it because we were friends. I didn't want it any other way. I had come too far for that and I felt we both had too much integrity to bluff it. I had seen gyms/dojos that threw belts at people for money, just so they can in turn open a club and make their Instructor richer. It is dangerous and unethical.

Geoff then told me that I had to 'survive' the grading to pass. If for any reason I gave up or couldn't continue because of injury then I would have to come back and complete the grading at another time, or I would fail.

I would not give up, I knew that much. I had come too far and had to much to lose to give up. This was my Frank Bruno versus Mike Tyson (and we all know what happened to Mr Bruno, as brave and courageous as he was!).

My first fight would be against Justin. As we came onto the mats, we touched gloves and off we went. For a few rounds I felt comfortable and was throwing some nice kicks and punches, holding my own and looking, as I was later told by Geoff, 'class'. And that's the last thing I remember...

In the debrief afterwards I was told that Justin threw a "spiteful" wicked hook and knocked me cold out. What happened next is still lost on me to this day, save for a few snippets here and there.

I have been told that I was "out" for about a minute and put in the recovery position. Julie told me Geoff rubbed my back and talked to me bringing, me around. I stood on wobbly legs, totally out of it. Geoff asked if I wanted to go on. There was still a lot of fighting to be done, many rounds to be completed.

I nodded "Yes, I'm okay." What the fuck was I thinking?! Luckily, to this day I still don't know, but I do have to be honest, I think if I had called it a day there and then, and waited to continue the fighting another time, I wouldn't have gone back.

I had trained too hard, suffered too much and waited too long for this. Plus, pure and simple, I'm not sure if my bottle would have taken me to another trip just a couple of weeks later. For me, it takes a long time to train up to a grading and it's even harder to get my bottle up for it. It takes me months to batter my negative inner voice into submission and I have to start the positive thinking well in advance. To go back a couple of weeks later would be a bridge too far. I'd never get myself up for it. I had to do this today and so off we went again.

I don't recall what happened next but I do remember taking an incredible front kick to the stomach and went down again. I was in agony. Up I got and tried desperately to clear my head and get something going of my own.

I knew I had good skills but just couldn't seem to use them. No excuses, I was being outclassed, but in my favour I was damned if I was going to stay down. I was hit from pillar to post and then time was called. The fighters were switched and I was up against Lee. It was his turn to batter me!

I vaguely remember clinching him to stop his powerful head shots but I was so tired I couldn't keep hold of him. In the background I could hear Julie and Justin shouting encouragement but I was starting to come apart. I wanted to stop. I started to wave my hands to signify I'd had enough.

"No Simon, come on, just another thirty seconds!" someone, I don't know who, shouted. I was just half a minute from the end of the fights. I gritted my teeth and hung on, trying to kick Lee away.

"Time!" Geoff shouted, signifying the end of the bouts. The next thing I know I was standing by Julie and had no recollection of the previous morning or the events or of where I was.

I asked Julie where we were. I was looking for my Dad and couldn't understand why he wasn't in work on a Saturday.

"It's Thursday love, we are in Coventry," Julie answered, worried. Geoff looked on concerned.

"I think I need to go to hospital," I said with panic setting in.

"Do you remember just doing your grading, Si?" Geoff asked.

"No, nothing. I don't remember anything much. Julie take me to hospital."

"Simon, don't panic, you are alright, you have just had a nasty shock. Come on get dressed," Geoff's voice was comforting. Still dazed, I started to undress by the window in full view of the street below until Geoff and Julie pulled me away. They helped me with my clothes. And then I wanted to know.

"Did I pass?"

Geoff nodded and laughed, "You're alright then!"

I was delighted, tired and confused. We went down to the canteen where again, I was treated like a prize fighter. Tea was made for me, my bags were carried and I was given words of praise by the guys there. This had to be one of the most pivotal points of my life, one I will remember forever.

I couldn't believe a skinny little kid from years ago, who thought getting his yellow belt meant he could conquer the world, was…well right! I had conquered my world. I had stood toe to toe with some of the finest fighters in Europe, if not the world.

I had faced demons I couldn't imagine, not just the guys in front of me. I had beaten fear, persevered through months of waking up with it at my bedside waiting to accompany me through the day. I had sat with my head down the toilet, sick with nerves, my inner voice telling me I didn't have to do this, my heart urging me on, knowing that if I was ever going to make something of my life, that I did indeed have to do this. I had held my own, my nerve and now my head held high. I no longer had to prove anything to anyone, least of all myself.

After a short, much needed break from training, I was at it again. Full contact was a regular part of my regime. Personally, for me it was a great confidence booster and a way to test both my skills and character. But I didn't really feel the need to test myself anymore, not at this time anyway.

I started to question whether I should really be doing this much kind of training and looked for signs that would tell me I had had my time. Boy oh boy did God give me a sign...

I was always aware of how very dangerous it was and the danger was bought home to me one scary Saturday afternoon in the same envelope as the sign from God!

I was approaching the age of 34, an age when most fighters have already given the sport up. I still enjoyed the fights and was as sharp as I had ever been. The knockout by Justin is the only time I have ever been on the floor although I have both given and taken a lot of heavy shots in my time.

One particular afternoon saw me and two of my people having a heavy spar in the gym. After six or so rounds we decided on one last session. About halfway through the round I got caught with a lovely roundhouse kick to the side of my neck/bottom of my head. At first I thought nothing of it and carried on fighting.

A couple of minutes later time was called and we all cooled down. As always after these sessions, we sat on the mats and had a bit of a debrief and a chat. It was a sunny day, and the glare of the sun reflected off the building opposite ours so at first I thought nothing of it when my sight went a bit fuzzy. I just thought the sunlight had caught me in the eye.

I tried to blink it away but my vision was getting worse. Not wanting to worry the other two, I stood to leave, shook hands with them and made my way to the car. I was starting to feel frightened and wanted to be with Julie.

I could see directly in front of me but my peripheral vision was very blurred and I started to get a headache. Stupidly, I drove home and I feel revulsion when I think of the damage my actions could have caused that day. I was selfish in driving but was by now, very frightened.

On arriving home, Julie looked worried when she saw me. I told her what had happened.

"All underneath your eyes are dark," she said. "Perhaps you should go to the hospital."

I could hear the children playing in the garden, waiting for me to light the barbeque. I felt sick at the thought of what might be happening to me and didn't want them to see me like this.

I made my way to the hospital and by now the pain in my head was enough to make me yelp out. By the time I was at the reception I could see only a pin hole in front of me. When

I explained what had happened, the nurse looked concerned and sent me to a room where a doctor came to see me almost straight away.

He shone a pen light torch in my eyes and asked me a few questions. Then he told me to wait quietly, he would be back to see me shortly. I sat on my own for about an hour and had time for quiet reflection. In my mind I could see my kids sitting on their garden swing waiting for me, wondering where I was. The pain in my head was worsening and now my vision was fluttering.

My thoughts turned to my training and I was forced to ask myself was it all worth it. I'd had a good term of duty in the full contact game. Many years of getting hit in the head for fun. I had nothing to prove to myself any more, my health had to come first. How many more hits would it take before it was one hit too many? I willed my vision to return to normal and for the pain in my head to go away.

Promises were made:

"Please God, see me through this and I'll go to church every Sunday! I'll never think a bad thought or swear again!"

There and then I made a decision to pack in the full contact. It wasn't one made out of fear, rather sense. The knockout by Justin had been bad enough but here I was, sitting on my own in a hospital room on a lovely sunny Saturday, when I should have been at home cooking burgers for my little pals. If anybody couldn't respect my decision, it was because they hadn't been there. They had never experienced full contact of any kind. The people who had donned the gloves themselves would not think any less of me, and deep in my heart I knew I wasn't "bottling it".

I'd had my time. If I got though this then any sparring I would do would be controlled with the protection of a head guard. Anybody who wouldn't accept this could find another head to punch.

The pain in my head wasn't easing but, I noticed with some relief, I could see a little better. "Please God let me be alright!" I pleaded.

The doctor returned and did a few more checks. He asked me again what had happened and when I told him about the kick he inspected the part of the neck that was struck. My vision was returning, some three hours after it had first started going and I explained this to him. After a few more checks he gave me the good news:

"You've damaged your optic nerve. You'll have a bad headache for a few days and keep your eye on things, but you should be okay. If you get any complications, come straight back here straight away, okay?" he advised.

I nodded, agreeing to anything as long as I would be okay.

"How old are you?" he asked.

"Nearly 34." I replied.

"Bit old for all this fighting now, aren't you? Why don't you leave it to the young lads?" he said with a grin but I could tell by his demeanor that he meant it.

"Cheeky Sod!" I thought. "I'll give him some good news of my own in a minute!" He was right though. I could still have a good spar but just not full out any more. Light continuous doesn't hold the same thrill for me as full contact but it's enough, and the way my lads fight, it still tests me now and again.

I walked out of the hospital into the bright sunny afternoon with a pain in my head but a spring in my step. As I walked through the front door my kids threw themselves at me, grappling me to the floor.

"There's always wrestling!" I told myself as we made our way to the garden for our food, a few drinks and a lovely evening. ☺

CHAPTER THIRTEEN

The euphoria of the grading stayed with me for a long time. Although I didn't win a fight, I had stood on the mats with two of the finest fighters in the world and did my best. My bottle held and I didn't give in. I had developed fighting spirit. Yes I been knocked down but I had gotten up again. I had given a good account of myself. That's all I could ask. I was proud of myself.

Back home, the boys next door were getting restless. Our court date was approaching fast and things were getting more and more tense. They were 'upping the ante' in the intimidation game. I was told they were about to do stuff to persuade me to change my mind.

They should have something good up their sleeves if they thought they were going to do that. When I picked myself up from my knockout, put my fists up again and carried on moving forward, something in me had awakened. Something that you can't get though reading about it, hearing about it or seeing it. Something that stays with you forever and something that very few people ever get.

Some people call it spirit, some call it an epiphany others call it their way. I don't really know what it is called, all I know is that I now had it. It was going to take more than a bunch of druggies to take it away from me.

And so it was that one Sunday afternoon everything came to a head, a showdown and the inevitable threat of violence reared its head.

I had to collect one of my dogs, Jake, from the dog run. All weekend, a small black dog had been running up and down our drive, another stray from next door. It was winding our dogs up and gently shooing it away didn't work. This was different to the Rottweiler. This was just a little pup that should have been looked after better. It yapped at my feet and I reached down and shoved it away.

It yelped, snapped and barked at me. From the window next door a face appeared. It was Nick:

"You're fucking dead!" he yelled. My, my, this was a turn up for the books, he must have been high, drunk or both.

"Fuck you, brave boy! Anytime!" I beckoned him out. Enough was enough. It was time. It had been on the cards for years and the breaking point was here.

What I didn't realize was that this appeared to be some sort of set up. The front door opened and a small army poured out.

"Oh shit!" I thought. Adrenaline surged through me. I looked at them. There were seven of them, all looking menacing, threatening and 'up for it'.

I looked around for my back up and there she was. Again. Right behind me was Julie. No hiding in the house for this girl.

"Go inside, get my bat and place it just inside the door," I told her.

She just nodded and went and did as I asked. Think about it. Once inside the safety of the house, would you have come back out? I know grown men, supposedly hard cases that wouldn't.

She did. She came back out. After making sure our children were well out of the way and safe, she came and stood behind me. She would not let me down. If we were going down it would be together, but I got the feeling her faith in me was at an all time high. She knew what I was capable of. What her nice quiet husband could 'let out' if need be. She knew that the only people going down today where on the other side of our driveway, trying to stare us down as they started to make their move.

I realized that this would be life changing and that they would try to rush us like a pack of rats, violence being high on their list of priorities and so I turned to face them:

"Fuck me! What a brave bunch!" I made a big show of counting them. "Seven of you."

I looked behind and all around me, pretending to scan my backup. "Two of us. Don't fancy your chances much!" I tried to appear nonchalant and it seemed to be working.

"Wanker!" one of them hissed.

"Me? Me a wanker?" I asked, incredulously. "I'm not the one whose backed up I'm I?" I laughed as I singled him out "Do you want a go? On your own?"

He reminded me of every scumbag who had ever bullied me. Sadly for him, this wasn't twenty years ago. He wouldn't meet my gaze.

"You. Do you want a go?" I repeated. "No. Didn't think so."

Another scumbag made a move toward me, which I saw out of the corner of my eye, sneaking around my tunnel vision.

"Fucking back off! This is nothing to do with you!" I ordered.

It stopped him dead in his tracks, and he beat a hasty retreat. I eyed them all as they all went very still. They froze. Their plan of violence, made on the pedestal of drugs in the comfort of their front room had not taken into account the lunatic in front of them.

I *had* to stop them in their tracks. This was the animal kingdom. As soon as one of them made a move, broke from his spell and rushed toward me, then they would all follow. God knows what they were armed with. So it was important, possibly lifesaving, that I held them in their place by 'persuading' them not to move by belittling them, removing any control or power they may have felt.

"Well?!" I splayed my arms out "What the fuck are you all doing here?! Not one of you has the bottle for this, do you?" One of them smirked at me, a nervous smirk that I picked up on.

"I don't know what you're smirking at boy, there's your seven to my two and none of you are prepared to take a chance with me." I spoke with contempt and then moved in for the kill. I turned to Nick who up to this point had remained quiet.

"You and me! Let's fucking go! This is our row!"

He looked like he'd shit himself. He glanced around for backup or somebody who would do it for him. All eyes were on him.

"Never fucking mind your mates. This is me and you. Let's go!"

Three years of aggression, anger and frustration came out of me. If he so much as moved a muscle I would annihilate him and he knew it.

"Ah, everybody knows what you are like," he offered meekly "You'll go to the police."

"No, you have my word. Me and you and whatever happens, no police. I'll just fucking batter you!" I screamed. I had to push home my advantage, this had to end today.

He had nowhere to go. Everyone watched him or held their eyes down, not daring to look at me. I just stared at him.

"I'll have my day with you," he blustered. "Scrawny."

"I might be scrawny, but I'm prepared to do it with you, right now!"

He went quiet.

"What, do you think you are going to get better odds than this?!" I laughed. "All your backup and you still can't do it. You won't get a better day than this. Come on, let's do it, this is your chance!"

He swallowed it. He just didn't have what it was going to take. I did, it was that simple in the end.

"Come on," He said meekly to his crew "Leave it."

They turned as one and crawled back to the house. They looked shamefaced and embarrassed. So they should. Their big plan of violence, their attempt to frighten me and do God knows what had failed. It had failed dramatically. The 'family man' next door had shown them a side they could not handle.

I laughed as they trudged away, finishing off their self-loathing and cowardice with some final words:

"What a bunch of chickens! See you lads!" Nobody would look back to me. "Bye now!"

They slammed their door shut and the house went quiet. I had defeated yet another demon. They had failed miserably in their attempts to frighten me, they had failed miserably in their attempts to persuade me to drop my case and they had failed miserably in their attempts to try and break me…they had failed.

I turned to Julie "Thank you." She hugged me as we walked back inside our house to our children. "I'm going to need a stiff drink!"

EPILOUGE AND AFTERMATH

Two days later I was driving out of our road and Nick's van pulled up alongside me. Him and his lot, held no fear for me anymore. Well, when I say 'his lot' they were no more. After realising they could not beat me, intimidate me or otherwise, they left...for good. You see they were the ultimate bullies and as I now know, bullies won't hang around if their intended victim will not allow them to dominate.

So Nick was on his own, looking lonely and afraid as he drew alongside me.

I lowered down the window "What!?" I barked.

"I'll pay you. Sorry. Sorry about all this...about everything. I will. Soon." He looked pathetic and ill. Gone was his bravado, for it is truly a brave man who can stand alone in the face of adversity. And he was just that, alone. Except he wasn't a brave man.

"You should have paid me three years ago," I said.

"I know. I'm sorry," he couldn't look me in the eye.

"Well the court hearing is next week. I'm still going. If you get the money to me in the meantime, fine. If not, tough."

He nodded again. I looked at him and knew there and then I would never see my money. He just didn't have it anymore. He'd blown the lot on losers, drugs and drink.

His life was in tatters and it was no one's fault but his own.

"You look ill," I said. Try as I might I couldn't help but feel some sympathy for him, despite it all. He was still a human being, still a man who had once been one of the good guys. I couldn't forgive him for what he had put us though but neither could I help but feel a pang of sadness.

"Yeah, I feel terrible," he said, coughing as he got his words out.

"Sort yourself out, Nick. You can do it. Get rid of the dickheads. They are no good. They never have been nor will they ever be."

"I've tried, but, well you know…" he trailed off and sounded utterly defeated.

"Put a few quid on what you owe me and I'll do it for you." I said. We shared a laugh, something we used to do a lot back when we were friends. That was then, this was now.

"I'll see you with the money soon, yeah?" I asked, trying to cut him some slack.

"Yeah, sure. I'll get it you somehow." This was the same conversation we'd had all them years ago when the money did exist. Now it didn't and we both knew it.

I drove away. He would make the usual excuses over the next few weeks but we wouldn't get our money.

Three weeks later his house was repossessed. The smack heads had long since gone, since the day of the big row. I later learnt that his parents had lost a fortune trying to bail him out. To be honest, I had little sympathy for them. I know we all want what is best for our kids, but getting the best for them also involves telling them cold, hard truths. His parents helped him hide his assets that could have been taken and sold in an effort to pay what was rightfully ours. I personally believe they should have spoken to him and told him that his behavior was wrong.

They could have then approached me and we could have sat down and worked out a solution, they knew I was a reasonable man. Instead, they chose to be clever and assisted him in denying us our money. In the long run, it cost them dearly so who is to say that they didn't get what was coming to them. No longer swanning around as 'lords of the manor', the father has gone back to work as a truck driver.

In our neighborhood, after I had broken the gang's spirit and back, peace was restored. People in our street started to smile at each other again. We slept safe, no noise, no drunks, no dickheads and no parties until all hours.

Some weeks later, The High Court awarded judgment in our favor. The papers were served on Nick ordering him to pay up, but still owing me the money, but he did a runner to the other side of the country.

However, through some interested friends, I know where he is and perhaps, when the time is right, I'll pursue him again for the money. Perhaps I won't.

At the present time, with interest and costs it stands at £22,000. At the talks and seminars I give, this story features predominately when talking about fear control, face offs and controlling violent people. I am always, always asked this question:

"Did you ever get your money?"

I answer, quite truthfully this; I got a hell of a lot more from the experience than what money would have bought. For one, I got this book and the story in it. This led to people wanting to train with me which in turn led to us being able to raise the funds for our full time centre, Simon Morrell's Black Belt Centre of Excellence. What followed from there was the opportunity to talk in schools and clubs about the effects of bullying and it is a very, very rewarding vocation.

A movie is now being made from this book.

I also learnt that when I had to be I could be a tough, uncompromising bastard, but only when I had to be. I raised my training to a level that would guide me through this conflict, a level that I would never have reached had this episode not happened.

My awareness level went through the ceiling. It had to. All these lessons, I keep with me, in my training, in my life and in my self-protection. I learnt never again to be bullied at the hands of another.

If at all possible, I learnt to love Julie more than ever. I managed to stay out of prison by resisting the temptation to take it to a physical level. No lemon was ever going to put me behind bars, for no amount of money, no matter how much they deserved a slap.

But most importantly, I kept my family safe. Today, I live a brilliant happy life, surrounded by the best people in the world. My wife and children smother me with love and I get at least a thousand hugs and kisses a day and I love and appreciate every minute of it and I thank God for it.

On my journey 'From Bullied To Black Belt' I made some great, great friends. I travelled to some great places and I have been taught by some great fighters. I have laughed, cried, been bruised and battered and very, very importantly, I learnt that when it mattered, when it really, really mattered, I had what it takes to 'dig deep'. Not bad for a 'spaz'.

God bless, He will do.

Simon Morrell

An Everyday Warrior

The sequel to From Bullied To Black Belt

Just as it seemed Simon's life was finally on track, a series of horrific events took place which nearly finished him off for good. Simon had to draw upon ever ounce of strength he had to even survive but could he once again emerge triumphant?

By Simon Morrell

"Simon is a Warrior, this book will help you become the same."

Geoff Thompson

A TRUE STORY.

AN EVERYDAY WARRIOR

The long awaited sequel to

From Bullied To Black Belt.

By Simon Morrell

"You have a month" came the strong Irish brogue and I knew even more adversity was heading my way. After answering to the sins of my Father just months before by paying his debt to a vicious gangster, here I was again, paying yet another of his dues. This time the creditor was, I was reliably informed, no small matter of members of the I.R.A. They were quite clear about my fate if I didn't pay up:

"You are to be put in the back of a van, taken to Ireland and never be seen again."

I had no doubt to the seriousness of the threats and the ability of the people warning me as to how they could carry it out. I did what I had to do. Simply shrug my shoulders, roll up my sleeves and get on with finding the money my dad had taken off them months before.

It would take its toll though. Months later my family turn their back on me blaming me for all and sundry. My own father even attacked me for paying his debt.

Drink was inevitable. I simply could not see how much I was hurting my own wife and children until it was nearly too late. Lying in a hospital bed and seeing my beautiful wife's face full of tears as she thought I neared death I knew I had to find the Warrior in me. The Warrior that had seen me through so much and kept my own family safe. The thing is, did he still exist? I was about to find out.

An Everyday Warrior is now available in paperback throughout the world at all good bookstores and via www.simonmorrell.com

It is currently being scripted into a six part TV series.

You can train with Simon at is academy Fight Fortress in beautiful North Wales, United Kingdom or host him for a seminar of talk at your location. Contact us at info@simonmorrell.com for more details.

49716994R00109

Made in the USA
San Bernardino, CA
02 June 2017